Cognitive Value: Choice of School and Motive

Tatiana Semenova

Cognitive Value: Choice of School and Motive

Olympia Publishers
London

www.olympiapublishers.com
OLYMPIA PAPERBACK EDITION

A CIP catalogue record for this title is
available from the British Library.

ISBN: 978-1-80074-925-2

First Published in 2023

Olympia Publishers
Tallis House
2 Tallis Street
London
EC4Y 0AB

Printed in Great Britain

Introduction

Success, a noun meaning personal merit in a particular business. Luck is the randomness of an event that has occurred, favorably represented by our consciousness. Throughout childhood, a child is completely dependent on adults who should give him a chance for success, and there is no success without education.

In this book, you will be presented with the opportunity to immerse yourself in the world of knowledge, feel your youth, or simply philosophize about how dependent and at the same time diverse our thinking can be.

Every time thinking about the subject area, I had to feel emotional interest and struggle with my feelings in order for this book to be informative and accessible to a wide range of readers. Due to the fact that I am a specialist in several spheres — medicine, psychology and pedagogy, I once asked my little son about which profession is more important, a doctor or a teacher? And as expected, he replied that of course this is a medic, because he heals and saves people. To which I answered: "Yes, it is true, but who taught him how to do it?"

In my opinion in the modern world the profession of a teacher is undeservedly belittled. But we must not forget that we are parents, these are the first teachers for our children, and we know how difficult it is sometimes to explain to them something important and valuable.

Freedom, a beautiful and unusual word. It has special meaning in this book. Knowledge in many ways makes people

7

freer, studying science every day, first at school, then at a college or university, you are getting closer to success.

And then the main question arises: Can study be free without rules, assessments and comparisons, without control, or is it still a purposeful controlled process?

In fact, this book is not really about school, it is about meanings and possibilities.

I.

Historical Outline

The development of pedagogical systems has its own history and interpretation. The beginning of its origin is considered to be the emergence of collective thinking among primitive people. Nevertheless, it cannot be excluded from the likelihood that rational thinking could have originated from many factors that cannot be scientifically explained due to insufficient information and the level of development of science at the moment.

Learning and teaching have different definitions, but their essence is the acquisition of knowledge through some tools.

In the process of evolution, people were constantly trained in survival skills and invented methods like tying a knot for memory as a way to transmit information to fellow tribesmen and their children — these are the first prerequisites for the emergence of linguistic communication, the main function of which is to share and transmit experience.

This first school was of great evolutionary importance, because it was the appearance of linguistic communication that became the main instrument of the transition of ancient man to Homo sapiens.

A human, like any living organism, has a number of instincts and reflexes that are genetically inherent in us:

- Food reflexes to subdue hunger.
- Protective reflexes arising from the effect of suddenness.

9

- Motion, grasping reflexes.
- And many more...

Separately, we note the so-called liveliness complex, (N. M. Schelovanov), when a baby, at the sight of his parents, tries to move, make sounds and smile.

But now the baby has grown up, some of the reflexes have ended their existence and for him and for his parents begins a very responsible period — the period of learning and communication — interaction with such a huge and exciting world through intuition, perception (light, smell, taste), tactile sensations (shape, size, material, temperature) and of course — speech. The first can and not — this is his first school and his first conscious lesson.

Communication of a small child with adults does not arise just like that, not by itself. It has its own time sequence and is aimed at meeting three basic needs (M. I. Lisina):
- The need for impressions. The big unknown world attracts the baby like a magnet — he is interested in absolutely everything at a very early age. Strange as it may seem, but it is the cognitive motives that are among the first to appear in babies, it is they that provide the need for new emotions.
- The need for vigorous activity. The activity of cognition of one's surroundings, in turn, forms business motives. The child is constantly busy with something, manipulating various objects.
- Need for recognition and support. Personal motives provide him with confidence that he is loved and supported. This is a very important aspect of child development — having emotional attachment.

And then it gets harder and harder...

Instinctive behavior is replaced by learning (learned behavior) and the turn of teaching comes — getting an education.

A preschool child needs a parent/guardian — this is his guide into adulthood, who must provide comfortable conditions for all-round development and in the future find him a school where the child is waiting not only for education, but also a full-fledged closed society with its own laws and methods of transferring information — as the primary task of education.

The choice of a school is the key to success, and therefore a relevant topic appears about what types of schools existed and exist now.

Let's dwell on different directions and authors as a way to understand and answer the question:

What is the ideal education?

Of course, the development of education is directly related to the invention of writing. In Ancient Egypt, the first written texts date back to around 3000 B.C. The Egyptians mastered writing with the help of hieroglyphs. The writing technology was very complicated and painstaking, the master needed a lot of time to draw complex details of the image on papyrus.

Also in the Ancient World, the Sumerian civilization invents pictograms — signs, images, which are simplified drawings of objects. Subsequently, the pictograms were modified to wedge-shaped signs (about six hundred characters in total). This is how cuneiform came into being. In addition, the Sumerians invented the wheel and made outstanding strides in mathematics. They introduced the sixty-digit system, now it is used in the countdown — sixty seconds/sixty minutes.

Further Phoenicians, complex writing with hieroglyphs is replaced by the alphabet (each character is a letter that corresponds to the sound of speech). Their alphabet consisted of twenty-two consonant letters.

In the 6th century B.C., Ancient Greece became a center for

art and education. The philosophers Pythagoras, Democritus, Socrates, Plato, Aristotle and their students created conditions for the development of education and enlightenment among the chosen children and introduced such a beautiful concept as paideia, which means upbringing, culture and education. It was then that the development of not only an educated person took place, but also the formation of a personality as a citizen.

Many discoveries of that time have not lost their significance in our time, for example, Pythagoras — the mathematician invented the multiplication table, the decimal number system and the famous theorem on the square of the hypotenuse.

Influenced by Greek culture, the Roman Empire realizes the importance of education and creates its own Roman school, dividing it into: primary, secondary and (higher — for wealthy families). Particular attention is paid to literature, poetry and oratory. In schools, teachers use papyrus scrolls, and schoolchildren write on wax tablets.

Paper appears in the 2nd century B.C. owing to the Chinese civilization. It was made from plant fibers. The isolation and mentality of the people of Eastern culture (expressed in hard work and accuracy) led to technological progress, which Italy and the rest of the world learned about only in the 13th century, from the traveler and merchant Marco Polo.

In the Middle Ages, almost no one except the ministers of the church still knew how to read or write. Starting from the 12th century, due to the rapid growth of cities, the first schools were opened, especially in the north of France. In the same place in Paris in 1257, the priest Robert de Sorbon founded a college (now the University of Paris). People from all over Europe come here to listen to lectures.

In addition to studying theology, students of that time could gain knowledge in the fields of law and medicine.

The English monk Roger Bacon — the author of works on physics, optics, alchemy, mathematics, (in which he described the structure of a telescope and glasses) expanded knowledge and set the prerequisites for the desire to develop science further.

Until the 15th century, scholars wrote their books by hand on parchment. The process was slow, time consuming and costly. In 1448, the German Johannes Gutenberg invented printing on paper.

The first book to be printed was a forty-two-line Bible with twelve hundred and eighty-two pages. Gradually, the printed book becomes available to everyone who can read.

In the 15th and 16th centuries, new research by European scientists caused a real revolution in science. The medieval purely religious view of the perception of the world no longer contains all the discoveries. Nicolaus Copernicus, followed by Galileo Galilei, conclude that the Earth is not the center of the universe and it revolves around the sun.

The new worldview of the Renaissance is saturated with humanistic trends. The head of European humanists, the Dutchman Erasmus of Rotterdam created his own doctrine — Christian philosophy, which was based on the idea of the relationship between man and God.

Today, the Erasmus program provides an opportunity for students from the European Union to study at any European university.

Well, it is to the Renaissance that we also must say thank for Leonardo da Vinci — a painter, sculptor, architect, engineer, mathematician, anatomist and astronomer all rolled into one, perhaps the most brilliant discoverer of truth.

The famous educator of the 17th century is John Locke. In England, a bourgeois revolution is taking place, which prompted him to create a pedagogical theory of the upbringing of the Gentleman. It was aimed at physical (bodily) and moral

(spiritual) education.

In the middle of the 18th century appears an another famous Swiss teacher, Johann Heinrich Pestalozzi. He created the Theory of Elementary Education, the main elements of which are — form, number, word. On this basis, the student must learn to measure, count, master speech. His activities contributed to the growth of folk schools and had a positive impact on the development of pedagogical theory and practice.

In parallel with Western Europe, from the second half of the 14th century, a spiritual revival began in Russia, at the origins of which was the monk Sergius of Radonezh. It made it possible to prioritize spiritual and moral education in public life and improve the level of education.

From the 18th century, a new upbringing and education began to form in Russia. New types of schools appear (from primary to higher), and educational institutions, both spiritual (in the 18th century they played a huge role) and secular. The significant role in the development of this education system was played by Tsar Peter I, Tsarina Catherine the Great and scientist M. V. Lomonosov.

Peter I laid the foundation for the modern education system, the opening of various secular educational institutions from garrison schools to the Academy of Sciences. In the middle of the 18th century M.V. Lomonosov raises modern education, there is a lightning leap in the development of Russian culture and science. With his name begins the history of the Imperial Moscow University (Moscow State University).

Under Catherine the Great, the system of Russian education continued to develop, and public schools were opened. New textbooks and teaching technologies appear in the school, including the classroom-lesson system.

II.

Author's Schools

Beginning in the late 19th century, the first pedagogical boom took place. In different countries, alternative authorship schools appear and are widely distributed. Unlike mass traditional education, these innovative schools were primarily engaged in the development of the child's personality, it's inclinations and abilities.

They were based on free upbringing, a movement that arose in the 18th century as a counterbalance to the forced school mechanisms. The first revolutionary, including in education, was the French philosopher Jean-Jacques Rousseau. He created a theory of natural upbringing, which takes into account the native nature of man and free development. In Russia, these ideas were continued by the writer L.N. Tolstoy, who believed that children did not need to be brought up and limited in any way. The child must educate himself and choose own path of development. The teacher only has the right to provide an opportunity to gain knowledge that is interesting to the child, and the teacher has no right to manipulate and coerce.

The ideas of the new education spread in Western Europe, where the teacher ceases to be an authority and takes an equal condition with the students. Let's describe in a few words the main pedagogical currents and their way of functioning.

In Germany, whole free upbringing alternative schools

communities were created (founded Hermann Lietz) — these are boarding schools built on the principles of free development of the child, compulsory labor and choice of educational activities. This system lacked a stable curriculum; civic responsibility was brought up on the basis of the principle of internationalism, since a fifth of all students were children from other countries.

The Waldorf School (R. Steiner, Germany). Emotional-aesthetic education and upbringing is the main aim of such a school. The training process is based on his theory of seven-year phases of growing up and developing children.

In Belgium, the Hermitage School (O. Decroly, Belgium) received its development — education and upbringing here was in close connection with the nature and freedom of the child, school, family and society. The training was organized taking into account the peculiarities of the development of children's thinking and interests, an activity approach was used: observe, measure, find, and think associatively.

The Modern School Movement (Célestin Freinet, France). He began his teaching career in 1920, in the village school Le Bar-sur-Loup, where only one teacher taught all classes simultaneously with all students from six to fourteen years old. C. Freinet saw that the main problem of learning is the lack of the ability of children to express themselves. This is how his first assignments appeared, in which it was necessary to write short texts on various publicly available topics, with a free choice for students. These tasks were called Free text, which had a dual function: correct grammatical presentation with a psycho-social context. It was children's creativity, where you could write about yourself, one's own feelings and plans and thereby develop an idea of the world around.

Then Célestin Freinet created a local printing house and the

texts acquired the status of publications, which before printing were checked together with students for errors, and these errors were subsequently entered into self-correction cards for better memorization. Such cards appeared in various subjects. The children used reference books, discussions and analysis, looking for answers to any questions. Most importantly, the students in C. Freinet do not know what error is. Here there are only misunderstandings, which are valuable, because having understood them together, you can avoid mistakes in the future.

As an educator and specialist in the field of psychology, I completely agree with the previous statement. Pupils do feel frustrated about the mistake they have made, not fully realizing that the correct answer does not appear immediately. It must first be found, worked out and consolidated, and then move on.

The Montessori Method of Education, (M. Montessori, Italy). Initially, her work was aimed at helping weakened and developmentally delayed preschool children. However, now this pedagogical system is being implemented everywhere in children of different age and psychological health. This method is used in many countries of the world, and a new specialty Montessori teacher has appeared at the universities.

In this system, the child is the center, he works in his own rhythm and chooses himself the zone and type of activity:

• the zone of real life, where the child masters everyday things;

• the zone of sensory development, where he studies the properties of objects (size, shape, color);

• mathematical, geographic, language zones;

• area for relaxation and reading and for physical education.

The task of the Montessori teacher is to help organize the

work using the motto help me do it myself.

The basic principle of Montessori Pedagogy is self-education; self-study; self-development.

Let me give my opinion on this method.

The first example, is the child who most of all loves to read. He goes to a traditional school where it is difficult for teachers to teach him disciplines other than literature. Suppose what would happen if he went to the Montessori class? According to her laws of non-interference in the learning process, the pupil would spend all his time in the reading room, without developing or showing interest in other subjects.

The second example, a child with hyperactivity, attending such a school will aimlessly move from one zone to another, without completing a single action to the end.

In our time, is increasing the number of infantile and weak-willed children who are not able to independently develop cognitive activity, and in this case, this technique will not contribute to educational progress.

If the ideas of free education were widespread in Europe, then in the U.S.A. prevailed the activity-based approach.

Renowned educational reformer John Dewey strove to bring learning closer to practical experience, that is, to organize learning by doing.

According to J. Dewey, labor should be the main activity around which scientific knowledge is formed. In his understanding, labor is a motive and a teaching method.

In the process of learning, their main aspirations developed: social (the desire to communicate), constructive (the desire to move in the game), research (recognition and understanding), expressive (the desire to self-expression, ability to use the acquired knowledge).

From this direction formed:

- Laboratory School (J. Dewey);
- School of Organic Education (Marietta Johnson);
- City and Country School (Caroline Pratt);
- Children's School (Margaret Naumburg).

The J. Dewey case is still developing. In 1991, his followers Ingrid Böhm and Jens Schneider — German scientists–pedagogues founders Institute for Productive Learning in Europe (IPLE) at the second congress the International Network of Productive Learning Projects and Schools (INEPS) presented a new theory of productive learning based on the principle Learning by doing.

After that began to open international schools, promoting Productive learning.

The essence of this direction lies in the student's independent educational work, which is based on the motivation of choice and personal preferences, together with real labor activity. It is not theory that is important, but practice — a material result, a real product, a training report, a project that can later be used in science and production.

The organization of senior classes in productive school looks like this:

- a group of up to fourteen people has a separate room — a training workshop, where there is a computers, printer, library, multi-media screen and furniture;
- individual curriculum — weekly, monthly, semester, annual;
- practical work (two to three days a week), in self-selected real workplaces as trainees;
- change of jobs every semester (up to eight places are obtained for the entire period of study);

- summary point grading system based on self-assessment and teacher assessment;
- preparation by each student of a detailed comprehensive report on educational areas related to this work, which reflects the individual acquired knowledge and literacy;
- teachers work as consultants in all subjects together with the students and the groups;
- flexible system of interaction between the teaching team, students, parents.

A very important, direction is touched upon in this productive school. How often do we adults, remembering our school, note how much information and work there was that had no direct relation to either the future profession or to everyday life.

It is more correct when the child not only learns the theoretical part of the subject, but also has the ability to clearly understand and see in practice its real application.

Of course, not all theoretical studies can be transferred to practice, given the tendency of young people to ignore elementary safety rules.

The school organized using the Project Method (W. Kilpatrick, U.S.A.) — provided students with a free choice of activities through which new knowledge was acquired. They also determined the content of the school curriculum. The teacher only helped them in this.

Dalton Plan (Helen Parkhurst, U.S.A.) — concept opens up the opportunity to study in an individual rhythm in those subjects that the student has chosen. The student group was of different ages. Initially, a contract was drawn up, which indicated the training program and the approximate period of its implementation. The school studied the main subjects: English,

mathematics, history, geography, natural science, a second language and secondary subjects: music, art, manual labor, home economics, handicrafts, gymnastics and other activities. Morning hours were allocated for independent work.

Nowadays, many schools operate in the world according to this pedagogical system. They are in Australia, Austria, Belgium, Chile, China, Czech Republic, Great Britain, Germany, India, Japan, Netherlands, Poland, Russia, South Korea, U.S.A.

Another American system that developed in the 1950s — this training on The Trump Plan. Its author Lloyd Trump, who introduced the lecture and seminar system used in universities into schools. L. Trump wanted to raise education to a high scientific level, which was just what the above methods lacked — Project Method and Dalton Plan.

In schools, his system worked in the following way:

• Lessons of the same time were assigned to lectures for large groups of students (one hundred or more students). Lectures were delivered by highly qualified teachers;

• The same time was devoted to individual work in laboratories, workshops, libraries. It was conducted by ordinary teachers, as well as classes in small groups, where individual topics of lectures were studied in more detail using seminars and practical works.

It should be noted that The Trump Plan system did not take root in mass schools due to the different level of knowledge gained in lectures and their processing in other studies. Schoolchildren were not yet mature enough to independently work with complex lecture material, determine their learning interests and choose learning methods. However, many schools use its technology especially with high school students in order to adapt them to university teaching.

It is necessary to draw a preliminary conclusion according to the above described methods.

Obviously, they are all united by one goal — to create personality-centered learning. It involves the use of a differentiated approach, focusing on the personality of the student, his intellectual and moral development, taking into account his capabilities, the level of physical and psychological health and interests, as well as other individual characteristics.

This, in turn, allows to select a more flexible educational process for each child.

The next stage of transformation of pedagogy as the main tool for personal development falls on the 1950–60s, when humanistic psychology appears in the United States.

Within the framework of this approach, a model of upbringing is formed, aimed at self-actualization and personal growth.

In the book Freedom to Learn, Carl R. Rogers denotes the purpose of teaching and education in changing the personality of the student as a result of independent learning, and the task of the school is only to provide conditions for self-development through the search for their individuality. The methods of upbringing are discussions, role-playing games, discussion of situations, analysis and resolution of conflicts based on moral choice. For parents and teachers, scholars of the humanistic school offer the following methods in communicating with a child: I am speaking, active listening, positive attention to him, eye contact, physical contact (for example, patting on the shoulder), empathy.

According to C. Rogers, the development of abilities, the search for the meaning of life is an innate gift and therefore behavior is explained by internal motives.

From humanistic ideas have grown a line of alternative schools in the United States: The Sudbury Schools; The Nova School (Seattle); The Schools Without Walls, and many others.

There is a list the general principles in these open schools:
- freedom in education;
- observance of democratic norm;
- equal interaction between teachers and students;
- to have the right of choice;
- the teacher must respect the interests of students, and develop their abilities for a specific area of knowledge;
- the students must carry personal responsibility of own progress in studies.

The ideas of free upbringing and other humanistic principles have not yet become widespread for one simple reason, the presence of official requirements and competition for admission to a college or university. Now, even in order to complete the courses of a teacher of early age groups, is required a school certificate with high passing scores, including in mathematics.

And for this in schools there must be discipline, ordering of knowledge and control. Great humanists were against these components, considering it coercion and lack of freedom and choice. But it is not so. After all, discipline is organization and responsibility, arbitrary behavior and self-control. As a result of these important qualities, develops the ability to make intelligent decisions under the strict guidance of teachers, the task of which is to structure the material, check the correctness of the tasks set and maintain a stable growth in the education of students.

The paradox of time — it is unlikely that humanitarian pedagogy will cope with these tasks when every year the curriculum in terms of load approaches the limit of physical capabilities.

Nevertheless, these schools have their own purpose. They are a valid alternative for children who, for whatever reason, cannot or do not want to study in traditional schools, but have a full right to receive an education.

And let it be better then it will be humane and free!

In Russia, a well-known pedagogical model is the system of Developmental Education (D. B. Elkonin, V. V. Davydov). In it, the authors propose to teach a child from the general abstract to the particular concrete.

D. Elkonin identified the following components of educational activity: cognitive motivation, educational task, educational operations, control and self-control, assessment.

For successful training, it is necessary that all components of educational activities are formed.

In the system of Developmental Education the main thing is the development of the ability to understand, reflection (introspection) and self-change. If a person has a need to develop his abilities, then this need corresponds to learning activity.

Initially, pupils carry out educational activities with the teacher, discuss and choose ways to solve the problem. It is in these situations emerges the Zone of Proximal Development (Lev Vygotsky). After that, each student continues to complete the task independently.

The concept of D. Elkonin — V. Davydov is aimed primarily at the development of creativity as the basis of personality. Many of its provisions were confirmed in the process of long-term experimental work, which was carried out in one of the existing school. However, this system is not yet sufficiently implemented in mass educational practice for primary grades.

So, we have finished the description of various pedagogical methods and author's schools, which are based on such concepts as personal growth, self-actualization, free upbringing, individualization of education.

III.

Traditional School

The main author's schools considered in the previous paragraph were interesting and extraordinary in their own way, they had freedom-loving views, where practically one person (the author of the methodology) wanted to change the education system, referring to its imperfection and relying on his life experience, intuition and desire to see children more smart and happy, free and creative.

History has shown that among them there were successful projects that still exist, but there were also less successful attempts that did not take root later.

Now let's look at what an ordinary school is like, which is widespread everywhere. A mass traditional school is, first of all, an Institute for the transfer of knowledge to the younger generation. It does not live an independent life, but obeys state structures — the Ministry of Education.

Here is important a rational, economic and social result, and not an emotional and personal individual approach. The predominance of reason over feelings, interests of the majority, authoritarian conservative views over creativity. And that's what peoples says after a job well done — it's not bad. This is the reality, the system, where many specialists create an educational environment to teach children around the world. This is the main task of the mass school, it historically arose for this. A few

centuries ago, education was of an elite nature, only children of wealthy families had the opportunity to receive a home education with a personal tutor or study in a closed boarding school. The majority of both children and subsequently adults remained uneducated, illiterate. But then there were revolutions in different countries and there was freedom, equality. The first schools for the children of workers and peasants began to open. These were just elementary schools, the purpose of which was to educate children in literacy, writing and counting. Well with this purpose coped Church schools, where religion was primarily studied. This was the first step to eradicate mass illiteracy and give everyone an opportunity to receive an accessible education. The era of enlightenment swept the world and formed a modern educational system, which is being modified to this day.

So what does the school look like now. The hallmarks of a traditional school are the annual classroom-lesson form of education, with obligatory attestation of students' knowledge. The organizational plan always contains such important components as: scheduled lessons, breaks between lessons and holidays. A lesson is a segment of the educational process, complete in terms of meaning, time and organization, and as a rule, it is devoted to one subject, topic. The work of students in the lesson is supervised by the teacher: he assesses the learning results of each student in his subject, and at the end of the school year makes a decision to transfer students to the next grade.

The class works according to a single annual plan, program and schedule. It consists of students of approximately the same age and is divided into several streams with either the same curriculum or specificity. For better mastering of the studied subjects, students use teaching aids and specially designed educational books that are for school and homework.

At first glance, all this is obvious and simple, but in fact, in pedagogy, there are certain requirements for a lesson:

- Using the latest achievements of science, pedagogical practice, building a lesson based on the laws of the educational process;
- Implementation in the lesson in the optimal ratio of all didactic principles and rules, effective use of pedagogical tools (diagnostics, forecasting, design and lesson planning);
- Providing the necessary conditions for productive cognitive activity of students, taking into account their interests and needs;
- Establishing links between different subject areas, the presence of a relationship with previously studied knowledge (following the achieved level of development of students);
- Consistency and emotionality of all stages of the educational process, the formation of students' motivation for personal development;
- Acquisition of the necessary knowledge, abilities, skills, rational methods of thinking, their connection with practical activities and personal experience of students.

Into account to these general requirements for the lesson are solved the didactic, educational and developmental tasks.

Didactics includes the plan and content of the lesson, the use of different forms of activity: collective, group or individual, the introduction of the latest technologies, management and control.

Educational tasks are aimed at the formation of human values, personal qualities (attention, empathy, tact…).

On development within the framework of school education is understood as intellectual, psycho-emotional, social development, the encouragement of creativity and interests.

To solve these problems in education, three goals are

distinguished:

- Formation of a scientific worldview, mastering the basics of science;
- Comprehensive and harmonious development of each student;
- Upbringing of conscious and educated people capable of physical and mental work.

Actually, this is only part of the tools that teachers use. In addition to direct teaching, their responsibilities often include: extracurricular activities, document flow, certification, security, accompanying students on excursions, parents' meetings, and so on.

In fact, classrooms are overcrowded in many schools. From this, the unbalanced load on the teaching staff is obvious. According to management theory, it is usually considered that a manager can effectively direct a maximum of five subordinates. Of course, this example is partly not correct in relation to children, but such a quantitative discrepancy negatively affects the teacher's work and the quality of education, since it makes it impossible to provide an individual approach to each student.

However, it would be wrong to assert that modern education bypasses and does not deal with the personal upbringing of students. It carries in itself the development, first of all, of intelligence, memory, attention, interaction with teachers, other children and their parents. This helps to identify the abilities and interests of students and allows them to develop those that are of great value. There are children who do not need the help of a teacher and they study well in mass schools, essentially doing self-education.

But in order to learn, you still need to study how to do it correctly and effectively. Usually there is not enough small effort

to change the situation for the better.

There are certain conditions without which training will not be effective.

You must be able to determine the purpose of your activity (for example, why you need to know the Pythagorean theorem). Next, you need an algorithm for performing actions, teacher control and self-control, immediate error correction, and of course the final result with assessment and self-assessment.

Separately, to this algorithm, you need to add the presence of feedback from the teacher (the ability to ask a question and get an answer to it, including on a controversial assessment).

In parallel with these conditions, it is necessary to form students' skills and abilities that have several levels and do not appear immediately in the finished kind:

• When a pupil begins to learn something from scratch, he does not have the skill to perform this action;

• Further, he gets acquainted with the rules for performing actions and learns to perform them with the help of a teacher or a reference book;

• Then the student does the work on his own according to the algorithm;

• Now there is a conscious solution to the task;

• A skill is formed — the automatism of performing an action (can be lost forever).

Formed skills and abilities can increase the efficiency of mastering of knowledge, enhance the motivation of learning, bring confidence and practical significance of the studied subject. It should be noted that what skills will work depends on the subject itself. For example, in technical sciences, such as mathematics, ICT, physics, chemistry, astronomy, you need advanced observation, logical thinking, the ability to measure

and compare data, use diagrams and graphs... In the humanities, it is important to be able to use oral and written speech, express your opinion and retell, operate with concepts and etc.

In the traditional learning model, students have to memorize a large volume of ready-made knowledge and most often this happens through cramming and repetition. Here we are talking about mindlessly coaching students into the correct answer, which is more suitable for accountability than development. With this approach, the situation is often repeated — passed the exam and in the next day forgot almost everything that known (of course, hardly anyone publicly admits this).

With a method where the student needs to create a project, solve a problem situation, show interest and motivation, in such conditions information is remembered better and leaves a trace, maybe not even the subject itself, but the process of its study.

All the same, in the modern interpretation, teaching is not just the transfer of ready-made knowledge, but a multi-level purposeful pedagogical process and the following features should be inherent in it:

• Joint activities of teachers and students. Education no longer carries a one-sided vector of cognition — I speak, but you be silent and listen. Now it is an alliance where the student has the right to vote, he can express his opinion, debate, argue and choose the direction that is closer to him;

• Teacher guidance should not be authoritarian and coercive, it should stimulate students to independent cognitive activity. As the humanists said, the teacher must teach the child to learn;

• Planned organization and management. Each lesson is structured in such a way that an inseparable holistic teaching is obtained, where one topic passes into another, without a jump of

ideas, using logical constructions from simple to complex;

• Of course, training should correspond to the laws of the age development of students, but one should not forget that the chronological age does not always coincide with the psychological one, someone develops more slowly, and someone faster. Children have multiple individual developmental characteristics, which must also be taken into account;

• Management of development and education of students. Yes, whatever one may say, the school is not only an educational institution, it is also the place where the child meets with society, communicates with it, receives additional development of his abilities and personality as well. The child spends a lot of time at school or generally lives on the territory of the boarding school, and of course, especially in this case, the school should take on, in addition to the educational process, the role of upbringing.

Describing the main characteristics of modern education, we did not touch on one point that is not directly related to pedagogical working, nevertheless, it is a new trend:

• Interaction between school and parents on the basis of digital platforms (not to be confused with interactive on-line teaching of schoolchildren).

In line with fashionable imitation and the desire for digital technologies, school administrations are actively moving to electronic, cloud and mobile platforms (applications) for interacting with parents, eradicating traditional communication (in the school, of e-mail). On the one hand, parents are offered the best developments in the IT industry. On the other hand, they are actually forced to agree to the use of such technologies, arguing that all school and personal information (reports, grades, photographs of students, signed contracts…) will be available only within these programs. Not everyone understands the

31

danger of digital rapprochement between schools and parents.

Imagine what happens if, by accident or deliberately, confidential or distorted implausible information gets into the school's digital environment for the purpose of a prank, psychological attack, or something else? What will happen to the family and children? Who will be responsible? And how can you prove who was to blame for the situation? How much will the school's impeccable reputation be affected?

Note that already now some of the questions described above have a negative impact on parents and on the entire pedagogical process.

Strictly speaking, there should always be a guaranteed distance between the school and the parents in order to avoid such serious failures. The forced tendency to transfer traditional communication to digital platforms does not protect the interests of children, parents, and schools. This is the personal position of the author.

In all this, the main thing to remember is that school occupies almost the entire period of childhood and adolescence of young people. Pupils come to school with minimal skills and abilities, then they will have a long way of learning, as a result of which new knowledge and ways of operating with it appear. The logical end of the school, of course, will be the opening scope of knowledge.

IV.

The Profession of a Teacher

The teaching profession is one of the most essential professions in the whole world. It is due to education that humanity moves forward, improving its inner and outer world. We receive all the initial knowledge from the teacher, and in many respects it depends on him whether we will have an interest in the learning process, whether our abilities will develop and whether we will find our vocation in a particular industry.

The teacher is the key figure in the school. He has been given the difficult task of teaching all students, including those who have no desire, motivation or ability for science.

The search for cognitive motivation and the desire to learn is a constantly changing process, especially among young people who, because of the stages of growing up, are prone to unstable emotional states. Usually people call the main motive for cognition — material values, forgetting the main purpose of education is knowledge for the sake of knowledge, self-development. In order to see this goal, let's try to get out of the role of a student and take the role of a teacher for a while. This formulation of the problem will help to understand what personal qualities of the teacher form his true motives for cognition. This experience is important both for professional teachers and students preparing to become teachers, and for parents, students, workers of human resources department, as well as those who are

interested in the questions: what is pedagogical work, what is its structure and functions, how learning activity is formed and what it is to be a teacher.

Pedagogical activity is a type of communication between an adult (teacher, parent, tutor) with a student.

Its purpose is to develop abilities and inclinations, in knowledge, skills in order to prepare an intellectual and moral personality, useful to society and to oneself.

Teaching is the transfer of accumulated experience, which has a stepwise organized structure for the formation of social consciousness in society during the period of development when instinctive behavior and spontaneous learning are replaced by a more complex educational process (with upbringing). Teaching a child is impossible without the participation of an adult, the Mowgli phenomenon is a myth, since genetic affiliation with Homo sapiens is not enough, and in order to become them, the influence of the social environment is necessary. Many philosophers, psychologists and anthropologists discuss the question: What is more important genetics or environment and what should be the percentage of these two components?

There are real life examples, when isolated children, with severe deprivation and lagging behind, scientists unsuccessfully try to socialize. This is due to the fact that for each higher mental function there is a sensitive period of development, and if it is missed, then the portal of humanization is closed. One of the most dangerous disorders in these functions is speech underdevelopment (the period when a child is able to master speech is only the first three years of life).

That is why we have a large number of children with advanced autism and other diseases, whose main problem is speech and communication disorders. This diagnosis is usually

made no earlier than six years, and this is already a missed period for the correction of speech function.

But let us return to the description of the structure and functions of pedagogical activity. Any science, including pedagogy, has theoretical knowledge and practical experience. The scientific theory of pedagogy develops and improves the principles of upbringing and education, which must correspond to the economic, legal, moral, ethical, national and psychophysiological norms of different countries, and each country has its own. Because of this, we are faced with the problem of employing teachers who want to work outside of own country, their knowledge and experience are not recognized and require additional confirmation, and sometimes complete retraining. The teacher turns out to be strictly tied to the norms and values of his country, which he has to pass on to the younger generation.

The transfer of knowledge, accumulated experience, the formation of skills and abilities entails the development of world outlooks among students, aesthetic ideas, the foundations of culture, moral aspects of behavior in society.

From the functions of pedagogical activity, which are similar in many countries, one can single out the formation of intellectual potential, abilities, emotional-volitional regulation and professional skills. Particular attention should be paid to the physical and psychological health of children. All these functions complement each other and are aimed at fulfilling the previously described purpose of pedagogy — to form a comprehensively developed personality.

The teacher in pedagogical work is obliged to take into account different aspects:

• requirements of upbringing which dictated by society;

- accumulated scientific knowledge that forms the worldview (meaningful attitude to life);
- knowledge of pedagogy, practical teaching experience, academic degree.

All these characteristics depend on the personality of the teacher, his moral, cultural and social position. I would like to describe these individual characteristics, which are important for vocational guidance for future teachers who are looking for an answer to the question: What abilities should this specialist have?

Of course, not everyone can become a teacher. In my opinion, there are two very important points in this profession: the presence of knowledge on the subject and the responsibility that the information studied will be used for good purposes.

History knows many famous scientific discoveries that have a double meaning for all of humanity. Let me give you an example of a controversy about Albert Einstein. Someone considers him a great scientist, because he formulated the general theory of relativity, and someone sees in him a short-sighted genius, since his actions contributed to the invention of nuclear weapons. The scientist himself, when he saw what turned out to be his discovery, said: "If I could do it all again, I'd be a plumber."

This example has to do with science and the possible risks of over-ethical disregard.

In the process of teaching, there is another component, this is the presence of confidence that your pedagogical activity carries a positive beginning in the development of the child's mind and does not injure the developing personality. Here, as among doctors, you need to be careful and attentive, using the law do no harm.

I will describe a case from my life situation. Recently, my

nine-year-old daughter told me that she was uncomfortable in science class when a teacher directed them to a film about conception and childbirth. And here's the question: Is it timely to show such stories at this age without consequences for the psyche? In our example — no! Many parents do not share such an early acquaintance with the intimate sphere of human life, but the developers of educational programs think otherwise.

So, we see that the teacher is not free in what information he should convey to the children, he has a ready-made curriculum developed by the Ministry of Education, with clear recommendations for its implementation.

Nevertheless, in addition to legal regulations, the teacher has professional tools that depend directly on his personal qualities:

• Oratorical talent, communicative characteristics: diction, intonation, voice, accessible presentation, moderate emotional involvement;

• Organizational skills: structured sequential construction of the lesson, comprehensive planning of the school day and interaction with parents, separation of field of execution assignments (group work, theoretical and practical part);

• Didactics: preparation of educational material, visibility, use of additional sources of information (posters, charts and tables, interactive tools). Ability to set purposes and find different solutions;

• Directly scientific and theoretical knowledge: the ability to research work, to constantly improve one's professionalism, to collect verified information from various scientific sources, memorize it and structure it in interpretation for a lesson form or seminars. Encyclopedic knowledge in various scientific fields and general cultural outlook. Ability to transfer theoretical data to practical application, use examples and associations;

• Psychological characteristics. As Carl Rogers mentioned, the main gift of a teacher is congruence, unconditional acceptance, empathy, that is, the ability to feel and empathize with his students.

I propose to consider the last point in more detail. In the teaching topic, there are several options for emotional interaction with students. For example, a cold, authoritarian teacher is not conducive to dialogue and cooperation. Children tend to reach for and respond to kindness. Yes, one must understand that a good-natured teacher must be demanding, fair, and persistent. He must be able to persuade and establish a trusting and tactful relationship with students. In his activities, he needs to use psychological and pedagogical techniques to maintain learning motivation, the development of cognitive activity, take into account the interests and needs of children, and also have the skills to work with lagging students, identify the causes and look for ways to eliminate them.

In the psychological characteristic when working with children, the teacher should have another important criterion — the presence of patience and endurance, emotional stress resistance. This is perhaps a rare gift, the ability to self-control, to remain calm on inappropriate behavior of the class. It should be noted that emotional fatigue and exhaustion is the main reason for professional burnout among teachers.

IV. i.

Emotional Burnout

The education system is constantly changing. This is due to the fact that it is directly related to the social life of society. As a result, experimental classes are created, new methods of online teaching are developed, public and private schools appear, assessment criteria and training periods are changing. However, these reforms often ignore the position of the teacher, who must adapt and receive additional retraining in order to meet the given level of modernity.

It is obvious that this reality most often has both a conditionally positive and negative impact on the professional and personal qualities of teachers. Intellectual activity, the need to restrain one's emotions, monotonous and extracurricular work, relationships in a team are part of the factors that increase psycho-physical stress and cause emotional maladjustment among teachers. This problem became widespread in the English literature when the results of a research of the so-called emotional burnout syndrome — a specific type of occupational disease of people working in the social sphere (psychiatrists, medical workers, teachers, etc.).

The term burnout was proposed by the American psychiatrist H. J. Freudenberger in 1974 to characterize the psychological state of specialists who are in close contact with clients (patients) in the provision of professional care.

Later in 1981, American scientists C. Maslach, S. E. Jackson detailed the description of this syndrome and developed a questionnaire with a quantitative assessment of Maslach Burnout Inventory (MBI).

They identified three main signs:

- emotional exhaustion (powerlessness);
- depersonalization (the tendency to develop negative attitudes towards customers);
- personal accomplishment (negative self-perception and lack of a sense of professional skill).

The following works of many authors dealing with the problem of burnout are devoted to the empirical study of the factors that can be involved in this process.

Personal factor — speaking about character traits (or accentuations), the most important are: *neuropsychic stability, self-regulation, optimism, active life position, sociability,* as well as *adaptive abilities*. It is clear that the higher the level of development of these qualities, the more successfully the individual can resist burnout.

Separately, it can be noted that the *value orientations of the individual* correspond to the work performed (for example, the teacher is forced to discuss topics in the lesson that contradict his religion and/or beliefs).

In teaching, an important role is also played by the presence of *individual prerequisites* and *demeanor*. David G. Ryans distinguishes two teaching styles — emotional (type X teacher) and academic (type Y teacher).

A type X teacher has a relaxed, personal touch, and a sincere and friendly tone of voice. He is usually an extrovert with a high level of empathy and achievement motivation. He is flexible in

his teaching activities, which may not fully meet educational standards.

A type Y teacher is credited with an alienated, highly professional approach. He is an introvert with low levels of empathy and achievement motivation. In his work, he is demanding of students and strictly adheres to the curriculum, so his style is more in line with the quality of work at school.

It is clear that the more pronounced one of these teaching styles, the higher the degree of influence on students, but it is not difficult to guess that the students themselves, especially in elementary school, prefer teachers of type X with an emotional style of teaching.

In reality, there are many variations in the types of characters and behavior that cannot fit only into the description of X, Y. Nevertheless, when studying the relationship between burnout and empathy (the ability to empathize), the authors note that both persons with a high and low level of empathy is prone to emotional burnout.

Work experience and *age* — teachers with long work experience and young specialists are susceptible to burnout syndrome. This interval is associated with the fact that teachers with experience accumulate stressful influences that increase the level of burnout. While twenty-year-old young teachers are still unprepared for professional activity with its realities.

Marital status and *gender* are also affected differently in burnout. It was found that women develop emotional exhaustion to a greater extent than men. There are a number of explanations for this: women are three times more likely to suffer from mental illness than men, they have a lower stress tolerance, which increases due to workload both at work and at home.

However, it is important to understand that such

comparisons (single/married or male/female) do not carry a balanced assessment, do not in any way promote modern ideas of equality and do not have a positive response from society.

More correct from the point of view of finding the relationship between professional burnout and interpersonal relationships (within the family, free unions, partnerships) is the scale: The level of trust. Harmonious relationships are usually built with good levels of trust and are important support in curbing burnout growth.

Interpersonal interaction. By creating own environment: social (personal and business) contacts, a person immerses himself in a model of behavior, where he often has to adapt to the needs (requirements) of a team and/or family. Such interactions may not coincide with own individual desires. A paradox arises, the individual himself seeks and creates his environment, but as a result he becomes dependent or influenced by close and less close people.

Motivation. In 1982, A. Pines and colleagues investigated the relationship between motivation and burnout. The following motives of labor activity were taken and analyzed:

- salary satisfaction — direct link between burnout and salary was not found;

It should not be forgotten that low-paid work strengthen to the emergence of dissatisfaction with life and as a result, burnout can occur as a consequence of the experience of social injustice.

- a sense of self-worth in the workplace — if the work is assessed as insignificant for oneself, then the syndrome develops quickly, and vice versa;

- professional advancement — dissatisfaction or lack of professional growth is associated with the development of burnout;

• autonomy and level of control from administration — individuals who lack autonomy in decision-making and depend on the constant attention of their superiors, are more prone to burnout.

Role factor — fair distribution of roles and responsibilities with equally normalized working hours and adequate material remuneration is an integral part of the successful performance of professional functions for employees.

When observed teachers and psychotherapists, were obtained data on the cause of the appearance of burnout with two concepts: *role conflict* and *role uncertainty*, which are very often interconnected (conflicts arise due to insufficiently competently composed job responsibilities and a mismatch of expectations from administration and colleagues).

This also includes professional situations in which joint actions are not coordinated (there is no distributed responsibility), where there is competition, instead of well-functioning teamwork (K. Kondo).

The incorrect balance of roles, silence about the full list of functional responsibilities, additional personal requests (to give a ride to the house, meet a relative, work out excess norms), all this contributes to the formation of a different workload. As a result, some employees are overloaded, while others, on the contrary, are insufficient.

Subsequently, both of them burnout: the firsts experience exploitation, fatigue, sadness and exhaustion, and the seconds — lack of demand, ignorance, rage and confusion.

Organizational factor — the school administration bears most of the responsibility in the emotional burnout of teachers and is

directly related to the issues:

- selection of teaching staff according to the posted requirements for applicants (not always taking into account the opinions of employees);
- drafting labor contracts, which should include important quantitative indicators (number of students, number of working hours and vacation days, salary);
- psychological atmosphere and discipline, regulations and student progress.

Therefore, the administration is the main initiator of organizational processes and is obliged to build its relations with all participants in the student environment in a friendly manner, taking care of the overall success and prestige of the school.

Due to the fact that burnout is a progressive process that usually develops in a stressful situation, it is important to identify how the employee responds to stress and what type of coping behavior they choose to cope with this difficult period.

Research show that those who respond to stress in type A: aggressive, competitive, unrestrained, are more susceptible to burnout; they feel a sense of depression, despondency because of the failure to achieve what they wanted (K. Kondo).

Great importance in resisting burnout and saving the health of teachers are active and passive strategies of coping behavior (P. Thornton).

Active emotionally focused strategies:

- distancing — changing the scale of what is happening in the direction of understating;
- self-control;
- search for social support and contacts;
- taking responsibility for what is happening;
- positive reassessment of values — search for the positive

in what is happening.

Active problem-focused strategies:
- systematic problem solving;
- path of confrontation.

Passive strategy:
- escapism — as avoiding problem solving, often via bad habits.

Active strategies that contain constructive meaning, contribute to successful professional adaptation and reduce the risk of developing burnout syndrome. Non-constructive behavior (passive problem-solving avoidance strategy, antisocial and aggressive actions) is associated with a high level of professional burnout.

IV. ii.

Help with Emotional Burnout

In the above factors, many reasons have been considered that contribute to the onset and progression of emotional burnout. Now let's explore the practical techniques and different approaches to helping people with this ailment.

Working with the personality factor

First of all, as strange as it sounds, we propose not to make hasty decisions, but to plunge into the salutary inaction. It is necessary in order to accumulate losses strength, to stock up on positive energy and to align your emotional background.

Only after that it is possible to understand the causes of this phenomenon, since they can be *definite* and/or *indefinite* (hidden), *internal* and/or *external*.

A *certain circle of negative influences* pertain events that can and should be independently influenced or eliminated within a short time (for example, discussing the problem with the superiors in order to restore justice).

An *indefinite circle of negative influences* pertain events that exist in everyday life as a given, and are difficult to solve due to the radical, sometimes absurd own position and the high cost of the planned event.

For example, someone is uncomfortable from:

- a crowded city;

- noisy office;

- route through an unlit street at night.

Subsequently, the individual himself realizes that some situations from an indefinite circle give in to a slow step-by-step solution, and move into a certain circle, which contributes to the exit from the state of burnout.

If you try to think about what really difficult obey itself to logic, these are such qualities of a person as: justification often repeated failures in the *providence of fate, superstition* and *prejudice.*

There are many examples when at first, people usually complete their inner cycle of activities (rituals) and only then are ready to start work with a good level of efficiency.

Let's summarize: in addition to consciously pronounced signs of burnout, among people may have hidden reasons that the person himself may not even guess about (for example, phobias and attitudes). It is important to describe a certain circle of negative influences and try to identify indefinite components and with this can help psychoanalytic techniques.

Professionals always recommend using an integrated approach — directed restorative process of one's own psycho-physical norms to the realities of the chosen profession, in which the circle of negative influences is narrowed to complete or partial elimination (reduction of the time of their impact).

Developing options for assistance, K. Kondo identifies two types of therapy: work with the patient and with the organizational factor.

Work with the patient includes various types of psychotherapy: H. J. Freudenberger's laconical therapy, and options of behavioral therapy.

Also, to reduce the risk of developing *psychosomatic*

disorders (insomnia, depression, irritability…), employees are encouraged to master the techniques of relaxation, autoregulation, self-programming.

With more serious consequences of burnout, when not only psychological, but also neurophysiological aspects are involved, it is possible to use medicaments (by prescription of doctor). Among the diseases requiring medical supervision and treatment the teachers, frequent ones are: ENT pathology, vision problems, cardiovascular and nervous diseases.

As commonly available containment and burnout prevention measures, consideration should be given to maintaining good physical shape and a balanced diet.

Need to try to calculate and deliberately distribute your loads, learn to switch from one type of activity to another, be able to organize your free time from work and have proper rest.

Working with the role factor

It happens that the reasons for an uncomfortable staying at work lie on the surface and not as much is needed to resolve them as it seems.

Yes, most likely if there are insurmountable disagreements with the team and administration or the employee constantly feels that he is not in his place, then the most optimal solution would be to change the place of work or type of activity.

C. Maslach gives examples when teachers, dissatisfied with the teaching process, felt their own professional inefficiency, but were quite successful in research work.

Working with the organizational factor

Administration can mitigate the development of burnout by providing employees with:

- Workplace safety and ergonomics;

- Allocation of responsibilities with well thought out job descriptions;
- Opportunity for professional growth;
- Quality employee relationships;
- Flexible planning of work schedule and short-term plans;
- Transition to a four-day working week for self-realization in new commercial and non-commercial projects, often not related to the main activity;
- The choice of the form of teaching, taking into account personal preferences (full-time, part-time, online);
- Supportive social and other positive programs that increase motivation;
- Conditions for professional supervision and support from psychologists, medical services, who are able to teach self-control skills and constructive models of coping with stress (emotional burnout);
- Specific regular trainings with information and advice on issues of interest, sports and cultural events, psychological relief rooms, leisure and other organizational factors that reduce stress.

Such work should contribute to eliminating internal disagreements, determining the true causes of the existing problem and developing an individual plan to contain or prevent emotional burnout.

Below we will consider several relevant psycho-diagnostic techniques that will help to identify the hidden causes and signs of emotional burnout:

- Maslach Burnout Inventory (MBI), C. Maslach, S. E. Jackson — general questionnaire for identifying three signs of emotional burnout;
- Maslach Burnout Inventory Educator's Survey (MBI–ES), C. Maslach, S. E. Jackson, M. P. Leiter — specialized

questionnaire developed for teachers;
- Arbeitsbezogenes Verhaltens und Erlebensmuster (AVEM), Uwe Schaarschmidt, A. Fischer — questionnaire for identifying types of employee behavior in the workplace;
- Psychological Stress Measure (PSM–25), L. Lemyre, R. Tessier, L. Fillion — the scale allows you to measure the level of professional stress;
- The Mclean's Organizational Stress Scale, A. A. Mclean — scale measures susceptibility to organizational stress;
- Ways of Coping Checklist (WCC), Susan Folkman, Richard S. Lazarus — the questionnaire is designed to study ways to overcome difficulties in work, learning, communication…;
- Strategic Approach to Coping Scale (SACS), Stevan E. Hobfoll — scale that determines the type of coping behavior in stress;
- Emotional Empathic Tendency Scale (EETS), Albert Mehrabian, Norman Epstein — the scale shows the level of development of empathic qualities: sympathy, empathy, friendly relations;
- The Ryff Scales of Psychological Well-Being (RPWB), Carol D. Ryff — measures six aspects of happiness: autonomy, environmental mastery, personal growth, positive relations with others, purpose in life, self-acceptance.

After acquaint these questionnaires, people experiencing burnout often have questions addressed to their personal, role and organizational qualities. With the deepening of the study of this topic, there is a desire to reassess the expected result, from the as is model to the as it should be model. In fact, this process of comparison can trigger negative qualities of a person, such as *envy*, *self-interest*, which is a false direction for getting out of the

state of burnout. If a person experiences feelings of rivalry, then it is better to develop the qualities of healthy competition and teamwork.

In other words, when choosing a way out of problems, it is necessary to use available ethical means that in the future will not burden the person and others with their negative consequences.

At the same time, teachers should move away from the classical model of upbringing students in the learning process, in favor of a modern teaching model, shifting some of the functions to the school administration, which in turn should regularly inform the school community about the existing regulations and planned innovations for which it will be possible to prepare in advance.

V.

Learning Models

Today, there are many teaching models that have specific mechanisms for introducing various forms of cooperation between a teacher and a student into the educational process.

In the classical representation, exists three vectors of interaction:

- Teacher —> Student;
- Student —> Teacher;
- Student <—> Student.

Depending on the type of these gradations, three forms of teaching are formed: passive, active, interactive.

The passive form is essentially lecture teaching, according to the rules of which the student plays the role of a listener and writes a synopsis, receives instructions and performs it. At the same time, he does not participate in the discussion of the material and does not show additional initiative. He often copies samples from the board and is content with the information he receives. There is no group interaction or active search. The teacher is the main authority who directs and evaluates educational activities. The student obeys the teacher's request and depends on his control and opinion.

With an active form, appears feedback from the teacher. Students ask questions, discuss the material being studied, freely engage in collective work, create new ideas and projects, and also

show enthusiasm and interest in learning in general. These classrooms have a more lively atmosphere where can speak oneself mind and even argue. Children learning with enthusiasm and creativity, and the teacher is a mentor and assistant. Here there are fewer absenteeism and tardiness.

An interactive form of training implies interaction and active involvement of all participants in the educational process in the creative work in groups, where students share knowledge, assist, complement and evaluate activities of each other's. Being formed is a very important component of educational activity — joint knowledge gained through collective search. The teacher takes the position of a coordinator in the organization of independent work of students, supplies them with the necessary scientific material (educational network resources, books, etc.).

All these three forms of teaching (passive, active and interactive) existed and developed over many decades until appeared the era of the computer. The introduction of computer technology has made it possible to create a new direction:

Programmed learning. This idea was proposed by behaviorist Burrhus Frederic Skinner (U.S.A.). For computers was written algorithms, which prompted to users to consistently follow programmed prescription. Programmed learning is based on main pedagogical principles. The material is given in small, easily comprehensible fragments (called steps). This is followed by instructions for the sequential execution of tasks (at first these were the missing words in the text that must be filled in), then the completed part is checked and the correct answer is given, which serves as a reinforcement for further activities and forms positive motivation, retains interest in the tasks.

Branching programming offers several options for answering to the asked question, taking into account the

possibility of incorrect answers. After choosing an answer, the student receives instructions for further work. Such a system is designed for the average student and does not have flexibility, creativity and individual characteristics. Therefore, later American psychologist Norman A. Crowder supposed that computer technology should in addition to the unified order of mastering the educational material, offer also personal training programs.

Actually, this did not have to be expected for a long time. Nowadays, the latest technology have become an indispensable integral part of the educational process. In pedagogy appeared direction learn by playing. Computer games help to create a variety of problem situations, develop abstract–figurative thinking, imagination, logic, memory and attention.

The main is that gaming motivation is combined with learning motivation, and at the same time, increases interest in the being studied subject.

With competent use of a computer, it becomes an indispensable assistant for teachers and parents in the development and socialization of the younger generation. The network is a limitless source of information. This makes it possible to improve the quality of education, to establish individualization of teaching, especially with unsuccessful students, who often miss school classes, and to organize more productive interaction between teachers and students. And most importantly, it gives a real opportunity to engage in self-education and development.

However, the use of electronic devices has its drawbacks and problems. First of all, they became obvious in today's reality when schools had to massively use online distance learning. Teachers note a decline in the quality of education, a lack of

group work and live communication. All along of working with electronic devices for many hours has a negative impact on the health of children and teachers.

As can be seen from the above, the emergence of the so-called parallel school has its positive and negative sides, which need to be worked out and corrected.

More details about the pros and cons, as well as the consequences of online education and computer addiction, can be found in the book Social Isolation and Exit from Quarantine, or from other sources.

Separate learning

Of course, it is known that several centuries ago there were only women's and men's boarding houses, so separate learning is not new, but a well-forgotten old practice. The opinions of experts on this issue are ambiguous — some are in favor, others are against.

What can be positive about girls and boys learning separately?

The first argument is definitely the absence of awkwardness and embarrassment in front of the opposite gender. In such schools, children have less paint on their faces, they are more comfortable building relationships with each other — the same interests and games, less intrigue and rivalry, it is easier to focus on studies.

The second argument is intellectual–physiological development, boys and girls grow up in different ways — girls faster. They are more obedient and diligent in elementary school, they are more often set by teachers as an example.

Teachers also note that the same-gender class is easier to organize and calm down, productivity in the classroom increases.

In England there was an experiment where it was found that learning progress in segregated schools is higher. Boys feel more confident and show progress in learning, and girls are not distracted by classmates and vice versa.

Opponents of separate learning see the main disadvantage of such education in the lack of communication skills with the opposite gender, which can have long-lasting consequences, since after school a different world opens up for adolescents. Especially nowadays, when children have the opportunity to meet and communicate only within the walls of the school, because street life disappears and it becomes difficult to visit each other (everyone lives in different areas, and it is not customary).

The school stay on the only one place for socialization, where for successful growing up it is necessary to be able to establish versatile interactions.

Supporters of separate learning also point to the flaw in their system and therefore in such schools, for eliminate the lack of communication, they organize many extracurricular activities (joint excursions, holding a holidays, communication at breaks).

Children need of full value development, with the help of which they learn to build their relationships from early childhood.

Joint learning is the main stimulus, an opportunity to learn about the breadth of society, knowledge, opinions, ideas, including education.

Already mentioned by me, Jean-Jacques Rousseau built deeply different priorities in gender education. According to his philosophy, a woman is creature that is dependent and narrow-minded. She does not need mental labor. Since those distant times (and this is the 18th century — the century of the Enlightenment),

56

there has been a colossal change in the understanding of a woman and her place in the state and business environment.

In many countries around the world, the topic of equality is actively discussed. Nevertheless, most of the responsible and highly paid positions are still held by men. And many families, when it comes to which of the children must have a proper high-quality education, give preference to boys, since they should be the breadwinners of the family. Historically, women are considered to be the keepers of the hearth, men are mammoth hunters. This division of responsibilities is a natural genetic component: the maternal instinct has feminine inception. But in the modern world to wins not who strongest, but the more successful. If a woman manages to support a family, and a man manage a household and raise children, then such cooperation is worthy of acceptance and respect in society.

Private education

A long way of teaching children in school is strongly interconnected with the expectation of success in adulthood and carries the risk of losing opportunities if during this period of time occurs a systemic failure. Wealthy parents most often choose private education that meets the interests of children and the family as a whole. This decision is due to the fact that there are fundamental differences between private and public education. Let's first describe the main positive aspects of a private school:

- In the first place is quality education. These schools employ highly qualified teachers. They are motivated by the prestige and pride of working in renowned schools, as well as by the level of salaries;
- Small groups are a separate big plus, teachers have the

opportunity to pay more attention to each of the students. Now that the time has come for serious epidemic problems, and social distance is universally mandatory, it is much easier to create the necessary conditions in small groups;

• The third point is the modern equipment and increased comfort of these schools. Computer classes, classrooms with electronic boards, sports and assembly halls, a spacious dining room with its own kitchen and a school guarded territory;

• In addition, there is an extended school day or a residential school. A wide range of activities is offered: music, sports, dance, creativity, field trips, and of course language courses with different developmental programs for native speakers or not.

Of course, there are different schools and most often it all depends on the administration and availability of staff, but you must admit that all parents want their children to study in a well-built, clean and bright school with all the conveniences. Unfortunately, not all public and even private schools have sufficient funding to offer such conditions for students.

The next step is to consider the possible negative aspects of private education. Such information indicating shortcomings in the provision of services is extremely interesting from many purposes (including economic ones), and should be analyzed in the business processes of these schools:

• Certainly, a private school is not available to everyone, but in the current economically unstable world, I would say to a few. Tuition fees are colossal and they continue to grow. Education is a long process, parents have to recognize and predict whether they will be able to pull such expenses for studying at school, understanding that after it, it is necessary to have free funds for to pay for the college and university.

- We see a large outflow of students from such schools and the main reason is, of course, the material component. As a result, children suffer who are taken from a good school, where they are already accustomed and they have favorites teachers and friends. Pupils end up in a different environment and experience negative feelings about changes, most often not for the better.
- Another disadvantage of private education is elitism, there is no place for special children with psychological and physical features. For such schools, prestige is a very important aspect, therefore, here trained children of successful parents who are focused on education, development and results.
- And the last one is the territorial issue. If public schools are widely represented and the road to them takes little time, then private schools do not have so many branches and transport becomes an integral attribute, travel time increases. This tires and depletes the child's body, especially in a metropolis where you have to get to school in a crowded transport or stand in a traffic jam for many hours.

Parents need to seriously think about this, whether it is worth spending so much time and money on a private school, especially if there is a good public school nearby.

At choosing a private education, it is necessary to take into account many important aspects, the most significant in our opinion are:
- Existence the school license and state accreditation for the right to carry out teaching activities;
- Accordance of the educational program with your expectations (exams, output documents, certificates, diplomas);
- A contract in which the interests of the school are usually presented in detail but the interests of the family are very scantily represented.

I will dwell on a relevant topic — education of children abroad. In our time, people have ceased to be stay-at-home and have gained the opportunity and desire to live in different countries and teach their children there. However, learning far from home, especially in a boarding school, is stressful. At any school, a novice child from another country faces certain difficulties, ranging from language problems in communication and ending with general rejection among peers. It takes a lot of time (several years) to fully adapt, improve a second language, and even study on it an already complex science. Not all children can safely go through this phase without consequences and nervous breakdowns, arise psychological problems — they feel like strangers, abandoned by their parents and alone. As a result, may appear difficulties with the acquisition of knowledge, poor progress and contradictions both with teachers and with peers.

Psychologists advise not to enroll young children in a residential school because such training deprives them of the main moment of a happy childhood — caress from their parents.

Experts have introduced a separate term Boarding School Syndrome. Among the special characteristics of this phenomenon are: emotional coldness towards relatives, a sense of isolation, irritability and a tendency to bullying; in adulthood — workaholism, addiction to unhealthy habits, relationship problems, etc.

For general comfort and development, it is better to choose international schools, oriented for all children. Such schools have the experience and the necessary pedagogical techniques for a more painless adaptation of schoolchildren from different countries: here always presented special classes of additional lessons of English or other languages and the separation of the entire curriculum (mathematics and science) into strong and

weak classes.

Students receiving an elite education have great opportunities and versatile prospects in the future, which compensates for the lack of parental attention and, in its own way, strengthens character.

Undoubtedly, British schools are among the better of international schools. Their advantage lies in consistency, high training and a serious scientific base (natural science, physics, chemistry). In addition, in an English private school, children are not only teaching, but also get upbringing and comprehensively developed. British education has always been associated with quality, tradition and prestige. English language is the international language in the world of diplomacy and business.

In England, public and private schools are divided into:

• Nursery school — accepted children from three years old;

• Primary school — schoolchildren from five to eleven years old. In addition to the main subjects, young people from the fifth year of study, begin to learn a second language;

• Secondary school — students twelve to sixteen years old. At the end of the ninth year of study, students need to choose two disciplines for advanced studying. At the end of the eleventh year, and these are usually already sixteen-year-old students who take GCSE certification exams and either finish their studies or go to college.

• College — the educational program is designed for two years and it prepares students for admission to the university for an already chosen profession, therefore, in addition to compulsory subjects (language, mathematics), specialized disciplines are studied for which the A-Level exam is taken.

Actually, it is obvious that the path to higher education is

very long and painstaking. As we already know from this book, North American educators, back in the 1960s of the last century, wanted to reduce the learning load of students with the help of author's methods (free upbringing alternative schools). Now it will be interesting to briefly consider what modern American education looks like now:

• The Public Schools U.S.A. — the most common (eighty-five percent). They are funded from school district budgets and are attended by children living in the area served by the school. Study to register a place of residence is a global trend, and it turns out that the child is assigned to a nearby school and does not have the right to choose another public educational Institution. The quality of education in these schools varies and is determined on the basis of nationwide tests. At the same time, study programs in U.S. public schools provide international students with the opportunity to learning with American students and receive a certificate of high school graduation (High School Diploma). This diploma makes it possible to further enter the college or university;

• Community Schools are private schools administrated by community or faith-based organizations that reduce students tuition fees. Community schools are divided into specialized and charter. *Specialized schools* offer advanced education in specific areas of expertise, for example as mathematics, science or creativity. At entering such a school, you must pass difficult exams. *Charter schools* have a community school base. They must have a license to provide educational services and they must guarantee a high level of teaching;

• Private Day Schools in the U.S.A. are very prestigious, like boarding schools, but they are few in number (five percent) due to the high tuition fees. Students spend academic time and

extracurricular activities on territory of campus, live in a home with their parents or with a foster family (practiced by students who study according an international exchange program). These schools offer a wide range of educational subjects, a high level of teaching, an individual approach to learning.

• Private Boarding Schools are elite, campus-based educational Institutions. The fees of tuition averages about fifty-four thousand dollars a year. The competition for admission is extremely high, and is comparable at such as Harvard or Yale universities. For students who do not speak English, many private boarding schools provide the program English as Second Language, which allows you to quickly master the necessary level of language skills for further education.

Educationally, each country has its own strengths. For example, in Germany and Austria, better teaching philosophy and mathematics; France specialized on historical and humanitarian cycles; Switzerland offers to study languages, tourism and etiquette; U.S.A. — finance, law, political science, economics, computer science.

But compared to the U.K., private schools in Switzerland, France, Germany and the United States have less strict rules and a more tranquil atmosphere.

Actually now in many countries can to find excellent education. However, it must take into account that not always international diplomas are legally enforceable in certain counties. Students who graduated from the university are faced with the problem of diploma homologation. This is not a simple procedure that can take several years. It requires two documents from the country where the diploma was issued. The first document is confirmation of the authenticity of the diploma with an apostille. The second document, an archive extract for all disciplines,

indicating the hours and the results of the grades. It must be translated into the language of the country in which the student wishes to confirm his diploma. Further, the university considers the submitted documents and proposes a curriculum, which is approved by the Ministry of Education. After successfully passing the exams, awarded a qualification (it may differ from the initial). But that's not all, in order to make your dream come true, to start working legally, you must have a work permit documents.

Additional education

The schools organizes educational and entertainment events for interested students. For many parents is important that in such extra activities at their children are looked after by professionals while they are forced to be absent due to circumstances.

There are many types of activity's with different purposes, we will list the main ones:

• Educational purpose — consists in doing homework at school (to consolidate the past material), obtaining more advanced knowledge, as well as corrective work with children who need additional pedagogical support;

• Psychological-developing — includes activity with a psychologist who works on the development of all higher mental functions: memory, attention, thinking, personality development, cognitive processes, motivation, the formation of moral and cultural values;

• Social, professionally-oriented — allows mastering the different world cultures and professions, gain theoretical and practical knowledge for self-determination, self-development and further selection priority in determining the future profession;

- A separate purpose of additional education is creativity: painting, theater, music, handicrafts (knitting, sewing, origami), cooking and much more;
- Sports and health — each school has its own priorities and opportunities. For example, for some it is football, basketball, volleyball, chess; for others it is rugby, cricket, tennis, as well as dancing or karate.

All these activities are united by one goal, the formation of a comprehensively developed personality together with the development of individual abilities and interests in each child.

It happens that it is additional education that becomes a priority and takes more time and costs than main school.

Parents need to carefully regulate the level of workload for their children, as there are examples when the second activity interferes and slows down the main school and this enforce to poor progress.

In elementary school, I had difficulty learning math. When I was enrolled in a music school (it was my aunt's initiative), my efficiency decreased, and it became clear that I needed to refuse these activities.

You need to remember that additional education in no case should be at the expense of the basic one, especially if the child is uncomfortable and complains about his health.

Homework

A lot of disputes and even protests from parents and children arise when it comes to the question of whether the teacher should ask homework. Does the child have the right to perform them in full or in part, or ignore this type of activity.

In my opinion, work at home is no less important than in the classroom, because its main purpose is to consolidate the past

material, to prepare for final tests and exams. The material under study in the lesson proceed into the area of short-term memory, and in order for the information to pass into the long-term storage of our memory, alas, needed system repetitions, otherwise it is unlikely to be remembered or will not be reproduced in full volume. And the more difficult and important the information becomes, the more detailed it requires — one hour in a class may simply not be enough for its complete recognition.

I am talking specifically about the consolidation of the material, and not about the independent study of new information, since I am convinced that this is the work of the teacher, and not of the student.

Another question is how quantity and how much time is needed to homework. Here everything is very individual. For organized and intelligent students, homework takes minutes and is not onerous. For other learners, the process of doing homework is very often stretched out for the rest of the evening, if not the night; this can provoke family disagrees due to the fact that the child does not want or cannot do homework.

A separate topic for discussion in the family is the dilemma: should parents control and demand from their child to perform these work, as well as to help him in this activity, or is it a completely autonomous responsibility of the student.

My own experience prompt me — yes. This once again emphasizes the importance of education, the child sees that family is interested in his work, which is ready to help him organize working hours correctly, provide additional information on the issue under study and explain those moments in which he finds it difficult (taking into account that the parent has the appropriate knowledge). It should be added that the parent can only show the algorithm for completing the task, and not do all

the work for pupil.

Great difficulties arise when the student does not have enough time to complete all tasks. This may be due to additional activities which ended too late and the adolescent have time only for dinner and sleep. In such cases, you need to negotiate with teachers about a more flexible schedule for completing homework.

The same situation is observed in schools in which students come home in the evening, so teachers should minimize homework (do part of homework in school).

As a rule, work which not completed at just in time, is accumulate, and this adversely affects the mastering of new material, especially if the next topic is related to the previous missed one.

It is good when a pupil knows the sequence of everyday affairs. Teach your child to use a diary with which for him will be easier to manage own time.

Classes of special educational needs

Due to the fact that my specialization is clinical psychology, then here I could consider questions related to Special Educational Needs and Disabilities (SEND).

Referring to the legal aspects of The United Nations Convention on the Rights of the Child (UNCRC), Article 28 — children and young people have the right to education no matter who they are: regardless of race, gender or disability; if they're in detention, or if they're a refugee.

The number of children with special needs is growing every year, and many countries are opening specialized Institutions and special classes (resource room), including on the basis of general educational schools.

For a clever understanding of what are special classes, we will describe their more detailed.

The purpose of creating such classes is to provide teaching for students according to a specially developed program, which should correct the existing features, strengthen and develop psycho-physical functions, compensate for deviations due to saved mechanisms and prevent the main disorder that causes difficulties in mastering the general educational program.

First of all, in the psycho-physical aspect, children need to develop fine motor skills of hands to prepare for writing, phonemic hearing, speech apparatus (need a speech therapist), orientation in spatial, coordination and dexterity, as well as higher mental functions: memory, attention, thinking.

In personal development, the emphasis is on the formation of an active position of the student, which includes arbitrariness and self-control of behavior, awareness of his social school role, responsibility and independence.

For the development of the motivational component, one should gradually replace game and external motivation (mark, gift) with cognitive motivation, encourage initiative and intellectual-search activity.

Special attention in special classes is paid to the main mechanisms of learning: setting a task, identifying cause-and-effect relationships, the ability to compare, generalize and abstractly thinking, as well as operate with the received information.

Learning activities such as reading, counting, writing, retelling are basic for the whole school. Students with difficulties in these skills need additional classes with specially educated specialists.

Diagnostics of thinking

In order to determine whether a student needs correctional teaching, psychologists conduct a thorough diagnostic, starting from carried out to check the level of intelligence:

- The Raven's Progressive Matrices (RPM), J. Raven — allows to check attention, visual–figurative thinking and logic;
- Segen's Boards, É. Séguin — research of the level of formation of actions and logical construction using a board game (for children);
- The Stanford–Binet Intelligence Scale (SB5), L. Terman — intended for the study of cognitive abilities in young children;
- Intelligenz–Struktur–Test (IST–70), R. Amthauer — widely used in German speaking countries, modern version (IST–2000R);
- The Culture Fair Intelligence Test (CFIT), R. Cattell, — contains non-verbal tasks in the form of pictures;
- The Wechsler Preschool and Primary Scale of Intelligence (WPPSI), D. Wechsler — indicate the readiness of children for early school.

VI.

Reasons for Failure in Education and Ways to Overcome Them

Definitely any responsible hardworking adult is uncomfortable to be witnessing when his child is showing low results in studies especially if the conditions for effective learning have been provided.

Reasons for poor progress can be many and usually they require constant adjustment throughout the educational process. They can be conditionally divided into personal (psycho–emotional, mental and physical) and social (school, family, economic…).

First of all it is necessary to understand what is related to the failure in learning. For this there are diagnostic methods in psychology, after which a plan of corrective actions with recommendations is drawn up.

Within the framework of this publication as a correspondence consultation, they are of a general nature, what is acceptable for one child may not be effective or contraindicated for another.

Now we propose go over to consider the common causes of difficulties in learning.

Personal

Prevalent behavioral feature which has a greater impact on learning progress and brings a lot of problems for teachers,

parents and themselves children of course is an *hyperactivity*.

In general, it is rare when a child is grows up quiet, slow, taciturn and lack of initiative. In terms of upbringing, these are obedient, calm children, they do not bother anyone, do not interrupt elders. For psychologists, such children cause alertness, since by nature child development should be active, rapidly changing, energetic. Inactivity can be a symptom of complex deviations, ranging from asthenia (weakness) to mental retardation and early childhood autism (Asperger's Syndrome).

Therefore, active children are good, this is the norm. The question is to what extent they can be active, and where this line ends and begins chaos. Hyperactive kids are unique. They are in action all time, them synchronic attracted by all objects, are often distracted, rarely when finish the task, sleep a little, eat on the go, because cannot sit for a long time or even stand in one place. This restlessness does not allow them to master disciplines in elementary school according to the general rules of the lesson. Most often, hyperactivity is accompanied by another deviation — *attention deficit*, with underdevelopment of which the child is not able to independently set different tasks for oneself, solve them, and at the same time control your actions.

Restlessness and lack of self-control — this are two main sign that, with other characteristics, to form Attention Deficit Hyperactivity Disorder (ADHD).

It is clear that in a regular class, their learning turns out to be difficult. They are not able to sit for half the lesson without being distracted and thereby interfere with both the teacher and the pupils. In turn, the traditional school, with its own requirements, enhances neurotic reactions and the situation is getting worse. At the same time, such children, with the correct individual approach to organizing the educational process, are able to learn. At home schooling, they have the opportunity to refuse

medication support. This result in twenty-eight families was obtained by Mr. Peter Gray, professor of psychology at Boston College.

In many countries there are various associations to support people with these particularities. On their official pages in the Internet, are available useful recommendations on how to properly organize lessons and leisure. It also there you can find information about are held seminars and online counseling.

For hyperactive children need to create a positive, calm atmosphere in the classroom and at home, more often them praise and encourage. Positive attitude and motivation for success — yes; criticism, constant remarks, ignore — no. This attitude is also necessary for ordinary students.

Anyone who works with hyperactive children should have additional knowledge about the nature of this disorder and have a practical arsenal on correction. It's not just behavioral problems, these are physiological, psychological, neurotic deviations which require a special careful approach. And if the parents see that the school is not able to teach and upbringing child, then it is necessary to look for alternative education. This may be another school with experience working with such children or home schooling.

Let's list the main types of tasks aimed at developing attention to increase its concentration and stability:

• Interest. It is not so easy to create conditions when it is interesting and enthralling, especially in education. Arbitrary attention requires concentration and volitional effort. Of course, if the child shows interest, then it is much easier to keep his attention. Usually, in that like help a lot textbooks with beautiful illustrations and pictures, educational literature with quantitative or visual comparisons, crosswords, snake mazes or game mazes

with small ball inside (designed to train attention, coordination, dexterity), and etc. In the formation of interest, the main link is themselves the parents, which should try to provide children a new cognitive things. Here necessary the quality related goods. The child will feel more confident and comfortable with this approach, especially if the activity are associated to the audience (art, drama, music). Educational and entertainment centers provide trial lessons where you can see what arouses at his interest, which is initially superficial, and with immersed study can develop into a whole hobby or profession.

•   Developing games. For hyperactive children, are better appropriate non-noisy and non-active games (they are so overly active by nature), and games aimed at effort on oneself, for example, when the child moves to the music but as soon as it stops he must freeze. Or games — say the opposite. On the question when need to answer yes — speak no, and then if no — yes. Edible/Inedible — need a light ball, to catch him if it is edible, and beat it if not. Developing tasks on paper by the type of proofreading tests (sign, numbers, letters), graphic dictations for arbitrariness, where dictation (for example, two cells up, three – straight, two – down) the child must listen carefully to the instructions and correctly to do sequence. Raven matrices, Schulte tables, are used for correction and diagnostics. In addition, are well suited and like children the drawings find the difference or find a match, as well as different classifications for generalizations combine objects into one group or vice versa, remove unnecessary, logical — finish the series in a certain sequence. From coloring pages, could offer the pupil unfinished or only half-drawn images, let first he finish the image, and then paint it. All these tasks are aimed not only at developing attention, but also on other higher mental functions: thinking,

73

memory, imagination. Use interest your child's. For example, he likes cupcakes, when you will be cook, ask him to carefully watch and listen to which the foodstuffs needed. Later, in lunch time may inquire from him does he remember all ingredients and in what proportions. It's the same with cartoons: And you didn't pay attention to what Minnie was wearing and what car Mickey drove in. After walking in the street, ask the question: Tell me whom we met today, did he have an umbrella or a hat?

Diagnostics of attention

Recommended proofreading tests:
- Toulouse–Piéron Test, E. Toulouse, H. Piéron — for determining of attention deficit, executive function and memory;
- The Bourdon–Wiersma Test, B. B. Bourdon, E. D. Wiersma — designed for determine the level of attention, fatigue/productivity, resistance to monotonous work;
- The Landolt Rings Test, E. Landolt — allow you to check the characteristics of attention (speed, volume, concentration);
- Schulte Tables Test, W. Schulte — assessment switching attention;
- The Münsterberg Test, H. Münsterberg — diagnostics of selectivity and concentration of attention.

In the methodology of measuring the level of intelligence, developed by D. Wechsler, there are sub-scales for determining the properties of attention:
- The Wechsler Intelligence Scale for Children (WISC), D. Wechsler — sub-scales on attention 3, 6, 7, 8, 11, 12;
- The Wechsler Adult Intelligence Scale (WAIS), D. Wechsler — measuring the level of development of intelligence in adults.

Beyond attention deficit, syndrome of hyperactivity may include another sign — *increased emotional excitability* (affectivity and impulsivity).

Affective outbreaks in the form of over-emotions: strong crying, screaming, hysterics, laughter, increased touchiness and stubbornness are inherent in all children. Adults often refer to this as childish caprice. But when such emotional outbreaks fill the whole childhood then to form affective behavior, which interferes with adequately learning and that needed correction.

Children with impulsive behavior as with accentuation of character are characterized by the presence of unmotivated, sometimes inexplicable mood oscillations. Even the minimum requirements and prohibitions cause them hot-tempered, conflict, which easily escalates into quarrels and fights. Appears affective contagion, children seek and demonstrate interest toward aggressive, conflict situations for what win back their affect. Such impulsivity is associated with the underdevelopment of volitional processes, self-regulation of behavior.

In normally developing children ability to inhibit affective outbreaks to be aware actions and subordinate oneself desires to social rules are formed by the age of seven. These qualities are the most important criteria for a child's readiness for school, and in Psychology they refer to the term arbitrariness of behavior.

It should be understood that instructions addressed to children are not an order, but just a wish, an attempt to agree in an accessible language for children respecting his own desires. In families, there are often situations when the themselves parents choose the wrong moment, trying to impose their demands.

Adults need to learn to be lenient and controlling one's own possible negative feelings caused logical and not logical actions of children's.

In opposite to motor hyperactivity and emotional excitability can be refers to a condition such as *asthenia*, which develops due to somatic diseases or reduced volitional efforts characterized by laziness, passivity and superficial interests in learning, or even the absence of such.

At somatic asthenia, the main cause for increased fatigue, short productivity, drowsiness is any chronic illness that depletes both the physical and mental strength of the child. Such children to look like distracted, sluggish, them attentiveness are rapidly reduce, which is manifested by an increase in erroneous actions at the end of the lesson.

In the psychological characteristics of asthenic children and adolescents, there are signs: shyness and fearfulness, up to the development of phobic disorders. For obvious reasons, they are pessimistic, prone to fixation on illness. Constant dissatisfaction with oneself and one's condition adduce to problematic communication with people.

In purpose to improve learning results, it is important to adhere to a fulfilling lifestyle, with social contacts, travel, entertainments. At the same time, it is necessary to maintain the daily routine. Parents should help one's children only in those matters where it is required, so as not to discourage the initiative of independent actions and decisions.

The next sign that we mentioned above is *slowness*. It may not necessarily be directly related to asthenia. Many children complete tasks slowly, not due to illness, but due to one's psychotype. They have no problem with intellection, they just need more time to solve tasks. Therefore, they do not cope with the entire volume of work, which must be completed in one lesson. The main injustice that arises in such situations this is a low assessment of students because norms traditional education do not envisage flexible approach. In this case, the school does not have a solution for these children. Transferring them to a

special class is inexpedient, but stay sluggish students in a regular class disrupts overall productivity and work dynamics, on them is exerted pressure, as a result of which an inferiority complex develops.

We would like what also these children to studies with comfort and showed more successful results, all what they need — give it more time, so give it!

For example, the student did not have time to complete the work on the lesson, then in the school regulations it is necessary to provide for the possibility of completing tasks on break (in classroom) or at home.

A difficult exam it is advisable to complete in parts, by intermittent into several calendar days.

From the point of view of psychophysiology, it is inhumane to always adapted students to the average educational system, needed to have alternative programs considering the individual feature of the child.

Another serious problem of school age — is *laziness*.

In the first variant: laziness appears as a consequence of asthenia, in which there is no psychophysical strength to perform many hours of work. It should not be forgotten that children with chronic diseases are forced to take medications, often a side effect of which is drowsiness, reduction in productivity, which leads to passivity and sluggishness.

In the second variant: laziness arises in the absence of the desire to do anything. But unlike asthenia, the main component here will be parasitism, lack of initiative (that is, a prolonged period of conscious doing nothing), which usually progresses to school holidays and non-working days.

There is a saying that laziness is the engine of progress. Many innovations invented by modern civilization have arisen precisely because to make work easier and free up time for hobbies. For example, washing machine, dishwasher, robot

vacuum cleaner and etc. Let's take a calculator, why count in mind if you have this device, but for the development of mental operations for children and adults alike, training of the mind is necessary, and mathematical computation should contribute to this. Therefore, offer your student tasks that stimulate thinking, for example, the method Exclude words (a group of words where one word does not apply to it), or vice versa Grouping (ability to create groups of concepts).

And yet, for most people, laziness is a pathological condition progressing in time, its destructive influence does not appear immediately, and with systematic inaction and disturbance of the daily routine.

The cause of this condition is a disorder of the volitional mechanisms of the psyche, when a person is no longer able to make efforts and falls into suspended animation.

The next link is depression, lack of interest in learning activities, and in life in general.

Most often, students turn out in a condition of monotonous complex educational work that must be performed regardless of the fact, whether they like it or not, and even worse when the main purpose of these efforts is not clear. Gradually, the demands of teachers and parents begin to be perceived as an obligation that interferes with the enjoyment of life, taking away free time and the child makes his choice according to the law of least resistance in favor of entertainment, computer games — ignoring studies, skipping lessons, not completing a whole lot of work.

Over the past thirty years, the world has formed powerful gaming industry with its own unique marketing, where even the old iconic characters find new life in the digital world. Such an exciting environment for gamers is starting to take up all of their time. As a result, the phases of sleep are disrupted, there is inactivity and narrowness of interests, and with it laziness.

From laziness getting rid is very difficult — it's kind of

another addiction as well as dependence to games or bad habits. Studying is a laborious process, there can be no place for laziness.

Adolescents who develop addiction become sluggish, apathetic, drowsy in class, or vice versa, too loud, cheerful, with incomprehensible antics, foolishness. Physiologically, they also have changes.

Them no longer manage to keep the learning process in dynamics, what previously aroused interest and brought satisfaction both in study and in communication with teachers, parents and peers, now becomes boring, annoying and causes protest, negativism, secrecy.

Negativism and protest — a common adolescent deviation having age-related reasons, but intensifying with an unfavorable course and manifested in the motto — I will do the opposite. It is resistance in response to adult demands, which do not match the wishes of the teenager.

There are two types of negativism:

• Moderate — refusal to comply with requests and demands, accompanied by wrangling;

• Bright — screaming protest, in the form of verbal and non-verbal aggression.

Most often, parents are acutely faced with the problem of negativism twice during child development:

• The first experience occurs at the age of three years, when children begin to demonstrate disobedience and stubbornness, reject the help of adults, suddenly realizing that they are independent. That is why Psychologists call this crisis — I myself!

• The second experience is associated with adolescence. Young people in search of the True Self begin to try on different social roles. The feeling of adulthood dictates them to isolate from parents and teachers, since now they are more not

authoritative.

It is necessary to have the ability to understand the true reasons for the protest, for this you need to be able to listen and hear your child, so that he has confidence that he will be understood, accepted and helped, rather than will not punish, restrict, move away.

In adulthood, negativism can act as a personality trait, be a sign of a psychiatric disorder, or be temporarily present in people dissatisfied with their lives.

Therefore, of course, it is recommended to timely monitor and resolve emerging crises in order to create favorable conditions for adolescents to enter the adult world.

Diagnostics of aggressive manifestations

• Buss–Durkee Hostility Inventory (BDHI), A. H. Buss, A. Durkee — the original version, where the authors identified 8 forms of aggressive reactions: assault, indirect hostility, irritability, negativism, resentment, suspicion, verbal hostility, guilt;

• Buss–Warren Aggression Questionnaire (BWAQ), A. H. Buss, W. L. Warren — version of 2000 years.

Social — School

Oddly enough, the school itself can be the reason for the development of student failure.

By importance first ranked are located *security* and *administrative–organizational* functions, on which depends the prestige of the school. The most precious what there is every person has is his health and life, so families choose a school for their children, prioritizing these functions! It is unacceptable for the education process to take place in tension and anxiety. One of the most common causes of discomfort is *Bullying*, a

phenomenon that absolutely any student can face. Ridicule peers can developed to students an inferiority complex, reluctance to go to school, feeling like an outcast. This is a problem with serious psychophysical trauma and this must be suppressed at the state level.

We strongly recommend looking for a better educational Institution at the first negative experience.

Generating errors from the *pedagogical environment* — in the process of work, teachers may have difficulties in terms of teaching lessons, as well as from methodological support, these include:

• the content of educational programs, their inconsistency with age, individual pace of material mastering;

• stereotyped and monotonous teaching methods;

• lack of control and praise;

• dismissive arrogant attitude towards students, not taking into account their needs, interests and, most importantly, opportunities.

Also may be bias along: ethnic, mental, or even external signs. It is known that some teachers have favorites in the class, as a rule, these are students who are good at all subjects, with a well-tidy appearance. Of course, for any teacher it is easy to work with such children.

On this theme was research, where teachers were shown photographs of unknown students and then asked to determine their progress. It turned out that an outwardly cute, tidy child was rated higher by them as a good achiever and gifted. The rest of the students received an average or negative grade.

In England and the U.S.A., to prevent bias towards students, the practice of changing the class teacher and a number of other teachers every academic year.

Another point to which you need to pay attention is the authoritarian overly strict style of teaching and upbringing of the teacher. Yes, as a rule, students in this class are quieter and more obedient, but this is due to the strict suppression of any manifestations of emotions and initiatives, the lack of feedback (I saying and you keep silent, listen, do). Such teaching is even more repulsive, instills negative experiences (up to the development of neurosis).

Very often, highly anxious children (this is thirty percent of all students) spend their school day in constant tension and stress, sometimes without even realizing why this is happening.

In the development of at such students, are greatly underestimated self-esteem, communication skills. When speaking even with a pre-prepared report in front of the teacher and the class, they experience embarrassment, pressure, anxiety, which ultimately negatively affects the ability to convey the necessary information to listeners. In the courses of oratory, was considered a similar case: when a teenager could not fully answer the teachers' questions at school, nevertheless, in other places he did not feel discomfort from the performances, explaining this by the fact that everyone at school knows him, and in other places no one?

The other side of this example looks sad, when the teacher asks if the class has questions on the topic, students prefer to remain silent even if they know what to say. Them are pursued by only one desire: what would to end the lessons as soon as possible in order to leave school and go to the home.

Carl Rogers imagined school in a completely differently — a place whither children run and do not want to leave. Agree, it would be great!

To reduce the level of anxiety, helps the method of auto-

training (by means of self-persuasion). For example, before the exam session, say out loud that you are well prepared and know the answers to most of the questions. Imagine how you answer in class, and in front of you there is a teacher who listens attentively and who is also interested in you passing the exam.

Diagnostics of anxiety

In psychology, there are specially devised techniques dedicated to this particular problem:

• The School Anxiety Scale (SAS), B. Phillips — contains eight factors: general anxiety, experiencing social stress, frustration of the need to achieve success, (fears of self-expression, situations of knowledge testing, not meeting the expectations of others), low resistance to stress, problems in relationships with teachers;

• The Children's Manifest Anxiety Scale aged eight to twelve (CMAS), A. Castaneda, B. McCandless, D. Palermo;

• The State–Trait Anxiety Inventory for children (STAI-CH), for adults (STAI-AD), C. Spielberger — scale of self-assessment of personal and situational anxiety;

• The State–Trait Personality Inventory (STPI), C. Spielberger — allows to identify the level of cognitive activity, anxiety and anger (for adolescents);

• The Taylor Manifest Anxiety Scale (TMAS), J. Taylor — personality scale of manifestations of anxiety (for adults).

But how can a modern school become closer to young people, if for several decades it has not been able to eliminate the unreasonable model of preparing and passing exams.

Surely you could hear from your children that in the past exam there were questions that the teacher has not yet explained or asked for independent study.

For example, mathematics: the problem of calculating the hypotenuse of a triangle, to solve it you need to know the Pythagorean theorem (remember, where the sum of the squares of the legs is equal to the square of the hypotenuse). So the students have not yet passed it, but it is already in the exam?

And here is another example from the same subject area, in which not the study of the subject is traced, but the banal coaching on questions: Mathematics — the teacher in the weak group prepares the final exams for his group and gives the same tasks for the strong group. And what do you think — a strong group fails this test, as they study a different program — more difficult, but with different topics and tasks.

A joke from life: a test in chemistry, result: one student only completed fifty percent — the whole class laughs at him, the teacher explains — and this is the best result in the group, now the winner laughs.

Bottom line, the whole class failed the test. Who is guilty? All students or still a teacher who did not fully clearly explain the material and did not check knowledge before admission to the certification exams.

It is understandable to all of us that the graduation program of the school does not have the same level of knowledge as the entrance program to the university.

Almost every applicant who is entering needs to get additional knowledge with tutors or sign up for preparatory courses (better with the chosen university with its teachers) in order to get guarantees of successful admission.

The question arises, why and what are we taught at school?

Isn't it for, what would after it we have the opportunity to continue our studies at colleges and universities without any problems!

This is why at all times we see pronounced inequality and injustice among students. There are children who dream of becoming professionals, but they do not have either money for education, or a sufficient passing grade, or time to study, since already in youth they are forced to work. And on the contrary, there are children, who have financial opportunities, but they do not strive for anything and receive a specialty only for prestige.

A family

Upbringing and family relationships also play a very important role in the formation of the psyche and the development of the ability to learn.

There are two types of disharmonious upbringing in the family: with *hyper* or *hypo* care.

With *hyper care*, the child is the center of the universe, he lives under the every minute control of his parents, who impose many requirements and prohibitions, imposing their attitudes and lifestyle — to learn the best of all and be a leader. Him has to often hears criticism for any oversight, he is compared to more successful classmates and is constantly monitored.

The situation is complicated when the opinion and views of the child do not coincide with the position of the family, especially when choosing a profession, where it is important to take into account natural cognitive abilities and personal interests.

In *hypo care*, the child belongs to himself, his even minimal needs are not fully satisfied, interests are ignored, from him is rarely require anything.

Neglect can provoke vagrancy and often such children are brought up by the street, with all the ensuing consequences (pedagogical maladjustment, asocial lifestyle...).

In life, there is another common unstable parenting style one in two. This is when one of the parents chooses a soft style of communication and indulges all the whims of their child, while the other (most often the father) is tough and demanding, uses punishment, even for harmless offenses.

Such styles of unpredictable parental behavior, as well as conflict and problem families, are the cause for the formation of aberrant behavior and a neurotic state in children, which is expressed in an unstable emotional background (more often in a depressive type with low self-esteem and uncertainty in oneself actions).

Socially disadvantaged and low-budget families need help from government agencies and volunteers. Children should studies in dignified conditions and be provided with all the necessary school supplies, clothing and food.

In the COVID-19 pandemic, when schools were closed, the entire public find out that for many children, free school meals are the main source of food for the whole day, which they have lost. It's sad to realize that this is possible.

Diagnostics of family relationships

We offering to familiarize with several thematic methods:

• Children's Reports of Parental Behavior an Inventory (CRPBI), E. S. Schaefer — studies parenting methods of upbringing as this is describe adolescents;

• Parent Attitude Research Instrument (PARI), E. S. Schaefer, R. Q. Bell — researching parental attitudes and reactions related to family life and upbringing of children;

• The Sacks Sentence Completion Test (SSCT), J. Sacks, S. Levy — characterizing the system of family, gender and office relations;

• The Interpersonal Diagnosis of Personality, T. Leary — determination of the psychological atmosphere in the family and

work collective;

- The UCLA Loneliness Scale (UCLA), M. L. Ferguson, D. Russell, L. A. Peplau — diagnostics of the level of subjective feeling of loneliness;
- The Rosenzweig Picture Frustration Test (PFT), S. Rosenzweig — aimed at studying emotional frustration reactions (for adults and children);
- The Kinetic Family Drawing (KFD), R. C. Burns and S.H. Kaufman — projective diagnostic techniques defining family and interpersonal relationships.

Having completed the description of several keys personal and social causes difficulties of learning, can proceed to consider a separate direction in Pedagogy, which originated from *Psychogenetics* — this is a research of the criterion of the influence of genetics on learning progress.

Currently developing computer modeling of the human genome, cloning and chipping of animals (creation of a cybernetic living being) with demonstrations of workable samples in the mass media.

It should be noted that *the development of intelligent information systems* also directly affects the abilities of people, although it does not apply to genetics. Already now, going on redistributed the labor market, some specialties are replaced by artificial intelligence (AI). Teachers use AI to check handwritten texts.

Let's dwell on the main question of psychogenetics: How two factors complement each other — heredity and the environment?

It's simple — the genotype (a set of genes) is transmitted from parents and on its basis under the direct influence of the environment, occurs further physical and mental development of the child.

In fact, everything is not very simple.

How many examples there are when intelligent, caring parents grow up aimless adolescents. And vice versa, there are children from disadvantaged families, who strive to learning, get a profession and create a harmonious family.

The research of the criterion of the influence of genetics on learning progress turned out to be a perspectiveless direction in Pedagogy. However, what caused the need to formulate such a problem?

Certainly, in the 1970s it was customary to explain educational failure to the genetic inheritance. Imagine, how unethical it is to discuss people, humiliate of personality every time pointing to the factor of heredity.

Pedagogy is aimed at teaching people using knowledge (structured information). The teacher must show respect, loyalty and equality to each student, that is, see in them a personality, not a set of genes!

So the question arises for what or for whom it was necessary to collect and analyze data on the influence of genetics on learning progress?

This data was apparently collected for some purpose related to the future generation of people. For example, on the birth rate of healthy children or social protection of children from disadvantaged families.

Nevertheless, the line between good intentions and extremes is very close: for example, this can lead to the prerequisites for creating people with improved abilities and dividing people according to distinctive characteristics in order to find more effective.

At the lectures on Psychogenetics, a question was asked to the teacher: If there was an opportunity, for example, to clone, the famous composer W. A. Mozart, would it have turned out to be the same talented musician? In response, she told us that it was unlikely. In addition to the genotype, it is very important to

reproduce all the events from the life of his parents and himself with all the details.

A small remark about the composer's childhood. Yes, Mozart loved his mother. In fact, who had a huge impact on the formation of the talent of the young Amadeus was his father Leopold Mozart. He was a violinist and teacher. The father oneself taught everything to his two children, and Wolfgang and sister Maria Anna never attended a school. From birth, the little boy was surrounded by the world of creativity and music. The father never used corporal punishment and raised the children through work, instilling a love to music. It is important, that in his son he saw a genius.

It should be noted that biographers describing the personal characteristics of the musician mention his childish spontaneity and hyperactivity, however, he had a phenomenally developed visual–figurative memory and he could remember the composition by listening to it only once.

Between the ages of eight and nineteen, he wrote half of his symphonies, and in his entire life created (about seven hundred works) much more than other composers. This is really where converged innate talent and a quality creative environment, which gifted us brilliant compositions.

In the 1950s, otolaryngologist, inventor Alfred A. Tomatis in his experiments to try to prove that the music of the Austrian composer increases the level of IQ. This was later called the Mozart Effect.

VII.

Learning Motivation: Its Importance for Success

Motivation is my favorite and studied topic in my research study of learning motivation in normally developing children and children with psychological developmental delay. In Psychology, with the similarity of the general approach to understanding the motive, there are significant discrepancies in some details of the definition of this concept.

Motive, it is customary to call — internal urge of a person to a given activity, associated with the satisfaction of a certain need. Wherein it is considered that in the capacity of motives can be ideals, personal interests, beliefs, social attitudes, values. However, at the same time, it is supposed that behind all this there are still the individual needs.

The most obviously they presented in Pyramid Maslow By Abraham Maslow. In his work Motivation and Personality (1954), he suggested that all human needs are innate and consist of five levels:

- Physiological needs (food, water, sleep…);
- Safety Needs (security, order, stability…);
- Love and Belonging (family, friendship…);
- Esteem (self-esteem, respect, achievement…);
- Self-actualization (development of abilities). A person should do what he has a propensity for. One person wants to

become an athlete or an actor, another a doctor or teacher, a third an inventor, and so on.

Later, A. Maslow added to the fifth level Self-actualization, two more levels: *Cognitive Level – Aesthetic Level.*

On his conviction, the needs of one type must be fully satisfied before when another need, of a higher level, manifests itself and becomes active. Wherein, the author noted that for some people the need for self-actualization may be more important than, for example, the need for love, and that some people stopping at the level of lower needs, not having an interest in the needs of higher, even with the satisfaction of the first. The cause for this failure he saw in the development of neurosis and in unfavorable external conditions for the formation of personality.

In my opinion, hierarchy of needs is a utopia. There are many known examples when a person initially has one motive so developed, for example, a motive for knowledge, that other motives and needs fade and become insignificant for their satisfaction.

The great Russian scientist Mikhail Lomonosov was obsessed with science, and cold and hungry, without love and family in persecution, he walked towards the only purpose — self-development, cognition and moving science forward.

Or here's another example, about people who want to become Rescuers. They learn to save people at the risk of oneself lives. And their main motive is to save lives of people, with sincerity and self-sacrifice, and not safety, self-actualization or fame and respect from society.

The motive is sometimes known to the subject, and sometimes it is hidden from him. Do you know what aimless behavior — this is the absence of meaning, the so-called field

behavior (Kurt Lewin). Remembered a little kids, they are launched into a room and they begin to grab and throw everything that comes into their field of vision. What is the meaning of this activity? For us adults nothing, but for them it is huge — they learn the world of objects, master object-manipulative activity, develop coordination and motor skills, as well as thinking. But at this stage, the meaning of all this is not known to them consciously, they have not yet developed arbitrary behavior — behavior with motives and goals.

In children, only by the age of seven, develop the frontal lobes of the brain, and appear such qualities as arbitrariness and self-control. Having played enough, the child becomes a student, among he formed the skills of obedience to the teacher's requirements, he is able to control his desires and emotions.

The game now does not fully satisfy the needs of the child, in its place comes cognitive activity, he likes learning, communicating with teachers and peers, feeling important in the eyes of his parents, and getting good grades. This is the formed *learning motivation*. I described the ideal option, which is based on the most important idea of humanists, the founders of developmental education — self-development, self-actualization, personal growth.

It is a positive motivation filled with positive stimulus. A student with such an attitude to the question: What is the meaning of your studies? Must answer: Me like to learn, because as a result of this I develop and change for the better!

Most of the answers will be within the framework of down-to-earth reality. I go to school to: gain knowledge; to talk with friends; not stay at home; have lunch and play during break; etc.

In adolescence, students are better motivated by studies in order to: enter the college or university, become a specialist and

find a job with decent salary, and also do not disappoint expectations of their parents.

All these are good motives and they should work both separately and together, complementing the learning activity with meanings.

However, during this period, arises a psychological paradox — at this time, when, more than ever, it is necessary to concentrate on studies and the choice of specialized disciplines, learning activity for physiological causes ceases to be leading and, as we see, it gives way to personal communication, the search for oneself and a life partner, that can negatively affect learning and motivation.

The variety of motives in a person and the way they are used are unique. Who would have thought that the educational process can be built on negative motivation. Here, to the question why you study, the answers will be as follows: so that my parents do not punish me; there were no bad grades and not being a loser in the class. This attitude is based on fear, increases anxiety and neurotic reactions, but unfortunately, such *motives* (*avoidance of failures*) are also present in learning activities, offering their own specific stimulus for development and growth.

The motives of the learning activity of schoolchildren can be represented by three interrelated groups (T. A. Ilyina):

• Directly-urge motives based on emotional manifestations of the personality (positive or negative emotions): novelty, entertaining, interesting teaching, desire to receive a reward, fear of getting a negative grade, punishment, fear of the teacher, unwillingness to be the object of discussion in the class;

• Perspective-urge motives based on understanding the importance of knowledge in general and the subject in particular: awareness of the worldview, social, practical-applied meaning of

the subject, linking it with a future independent life (entering the university, choosing a profession, creating a family);

• Intellectually-urge motives based on obtaining satisfaction from the process of cognition: interest in knowledge, curiosity, the desire to expand your cultural level, master certain skills, enthusiasm for the process of solving educational and cognitive problems, etc.

Thus, it became clear that the presence of motives is an integral part of our activity, and the presence of cognitive motives is a necessary part of successful learning. Even with an insufficient stock of knowledge and average intellectual abilities, learning motivation can act as a compensatory factor and urge the student to a purpose — mastering certain knowledge and skills. It should be noted that the formation of motivation is a process where at first appear cognitive interests, which subsequently, under favorable conditions, can develop into persistent cognitive motives.

So we came to the understanding that motivation has its own time frame (interval). Our fussy pace of life basically gives rise to us short-lived simple need and motive. People themselves are very inquisitive, and most often are not organized.

Usually speaks that in one day enough time for all matters. This is what we must first of all take advantage of. It is necessary to consolidate in oneself the idea of all-round development, shifting the schedule between: priorities in business and leisure; smart and creative; conversation and reading.

On the development of motivation is influenced by many factors and, as noted by Kurt Lewin, they are very individual and sometimes hidden even for the subject himself. Among each person has his own meaning that he invests in order to achieve the purpose.

Therefore, the proposed recommendations cannot take into account the entire complex spectrum development of motivation and are only general for a psychologically stable personality with clear motives and purpose. But as the scientist believed, there are no such people. We all have different goals, and even if they coincide, we still follow different paths, because have different conditions for achieving them.

If the driving force is large and restraint factors are absent,

then you can reach your goal very quickly. Motivation is increasing due to the tension which arises when expectations do not coincide with reality and this state of tone forces us to move forward until the goal is achieved (this is the *achievement motivation*). This is how K. Lewin saw it, and I adhere to this theory.

According to legend, once K. Lewin and his student B. Zeigarnik were sitting in a cafe and they were interested in the waiter, who did not write down the orders of visitors, but accurately brought and arranged dishes for them. However, when the observers asked to name what the ordered, couple leaving the cafe, their waiter said that had no idea, because they had already paid. The action is over, the result is achieved and a tense quasi-need — remembering the order was successfully resolved.

This is how was formed the known Zeigarnik effect, which later experimentally confirmed the hypothesis that incomplete, interrupted actions are remembered better.

The Zeigarnik effect property can be used in training. Divide the learning material into several blocks, do not carry out the whole front of work at once, as a result, you may have a quasi-need to complete the action and this information will be remembered in a fuller volume.

But for people with increased anxiety and/or high rates in

achieving the purpose, such an unfinished action can provoke neurosis, insomnia and worries.

If you think about it more broadly, in life there is everything the other way around: did not call back, did not send e-mail, did not specify the schedule, and so on, although everyone knows the work very well. Here's a simple example of people who forget to turn off the lights in rooms. There is an unfinished action that should be well remembered, and it is in their interests (saving electricity, safety, ecology), but it is not completed!

So, in order to increase your organizational skills, you need to develop memory and attention, show interest and not initiated too many actions.

You probably know that memorized learning material without understanding is forgotten very quickly and does not carry an information load, because here used mechanical short-term memory, but at memorization based on associations and positive is much better.

I will give examples of some mnemonic techniques:

1) Psychologists A. Luria, L. Vygotsky and N. Leontev proposed a method of mediated memorization. The subjects were given pictures and named words for memorization that could be associated with them. For example, the word time is a picture of an alarm clock. It turned out that such memorization shows sufficient efficiency in the case of a mentally healthy person with well-developed visual–figurative and verbal–logical thinking. Use this *associative memory* it really works. Even boring and complex numbers will be easier to remember if you break them down into components like this: 2049, 20 is your birthday, and 49 is a number that is less than 50 by one.

2) The Hermann Ebbinghaus method is based on meaningful

memorization. This German psychologist has determined that memorization with meaning is nine times more effective than without him. Indeed, exciting information is remembered faster and for a long time than boring and uninteresting. The complexity of this approach consist of in the fact that for most schoolchildren, scientific information is rarely interesting. Also H. Ebbinghaus proposed an algorithm for memorizing in time, and deduced a forgetting curve. The algorithm is quite simple — repeat the material through a certain period of time and success awaits you (already on three to four days, a high level of memorization is achieved).

Serial-position effect. The scientist deduced a pattern that the first and last words are best remembered from the list. Use this, learn more important and difficult questions at the beginning and at the end of exam preparation. True, the serial-position effect will not always work, if in the middle will be a touched upon important for a person topic, which causes among him strong emotions, then he will remember it in any case. Will work an another type of memory — *emotional*.

3) The Feynman Technique By Richard Feynman. This Nobel laureate proposed a technique for composing interesting, simple stories from scientific literature. Compose texts (you can even with heroes), retell them in accessible language aloud to friends or to yourself. Try to explain the material clearly by introducing yourself as a teacher. This technique improves memorization.

4) Gestalt, from general to particular, from synthesis to analysis. Our brain perceives the whole picture better than its component parts. Therefore, when studying, first read the general patterns, the entire text, and then move on to the details (dates, events, step-by-step actions). Use alternation tactics. More often

change the type of activity and subject of study. It will bring variety to monotony and stimulate different thought mechanisms. For example, at first study history for thirty minutes, then mathematics, then chemistry. Break large volume into logically complete blocks, they are easier to master and easier to repeat.

In another way, (using the Zeigarnik method), divide the information not in a logical ending, but halfway. So you will want to finish what you started as soon as possible and this information will be remembered better.

5) Use different types of memory. Some have better developed *auditory memory*. Use audio lessons, read more aloud.

Others have associative memory. Looking for what information can be learned with the help of it, for example: comparisons, rhyming, imagery. Scientifically proven fact: our brains are better at mastering information received through vision. By my example, I say that this is my type. During the exams, before my eyes appeared a whole lecture on the required question, and I reproduced it on a blank page almost word for word. This is the so-called *photographic memory*. If you or your child is also visual, use schematization, drawings and visual–figurative projections.

Diagnostics of memory

The origins of the study of short-term memory are the following famous scientists with their research:

• Methods: Memorization, Recognition, Anticipation, Savings, H. Ebbinghaus — are used to identify the level of speech development, the productivity of associations;

• Digit Span, Joseph Jacobs — determination of the volume of short-term memory;

• The Miller's formula: 7+–2, G. A. Miller — the average

number of characters that a person can remember;

- The Method of Memorizing 10 Words, A. R. Luria — assessment of memory, fatigue, activity, attention;
- The Method of Random Access Memory, A. R. Luria — used to study the level of development of short-term memory;
- The Method of Pictograms, A. R. Luria — study of mediated memorization (associative memory).

The already become classic Yerkes–Dodson Law (R. M. Yerkes, J. D. Dodson), formulated several decades ago, establishes the dependence of the effectiveness of activity on strength (*level of arousal*). It follows from it that the higher the level of arousal, the higher the *efficiency of performance*. But the direct connection remains only up to a certain limit. Then some optimal level is reached. And with a further increase in strength (level of arousal), there is a decrease in the efficiency of activity associated with overstrain, fatigue, stress.

See below graph №1.

Efficiency of Performance

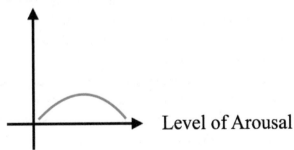

Level of Arousal

Graph №1. Dependence of the effectiveness of activity on strength (level of arousal)

Paradoxically, some experts use Yerkes–Dodson Law, replacing level of arousal with the concept of level of motivation!

In motivation, everything is much more complicated; in our opinion, it is independent of effective and efficient activities. There are many people who study or work without any motivation and are very effective! And there are people who are motivated and have no result.

Here are some practical examples:

• The student is highly motivated to master the guitar and has been training with a tutor for several years. In the end, he couldn't learned to play. The record company did not consider his candidacy and sign the contract. The level of motivation has not disappeared even after several years, but there is no result and efficiency.

• A similar example can be seen in the visual arts. The artist painted thousands of pictures, but as a result he never became famous! He maintains a high level of motivation but his paintings nobody needs?

• In learning a foreign language, you can raise your motivation to any level and even accumulate vocabulary (for someone it is a necessity, a dream, or all together). But in the end, not everyone will be able to use it (to hear, understand the interlocutor, build a sentence and respond), which means there is no result and efficiency.

Motivation is a subjective, rather a dynamic value ranging from neutral (when there is it none) to positive.

The effectiveness of activities is measured by the result and can have negative values both at the initial stage and throughout the time.

• Example with conditional: I want to go to work and want to sell a luxury home! Yes, I have a high level of motivation, Yes, I go to work every day — that's a fact, but I have never sold a luxurious house! The efficiency of activity is negative (no

income, only loss), and the result is zero (the house is not sold).

• By the way, in the example of the sale of a luxury house, there may be another situation when the realtor himself is not motivated at all to sell a large house, since, in his opinion, such houses destroy the ecology of our planet. But a buyer came to him and he had to sell such a house! There is no motivation at all, the efficiency is positive (income has appeared), there is a result (the house is sold).

At the end of the series of these examples, I would like to note that there are many professions where employees are given orders and it does not matter at all whether the subordinate has motivation or not, the main thing is to follow the order, show the result and effectiveness.

Now let's look at what factors lead to regression of learning motivation:

• lack of formation of target attitudes — unwillingness to learn in the first place, associated with not realizing what it is for;

• lack of healthy intellectual competition in everyday communication among peers and in the family;

• increased attention and control, increased requirements;

• overestimated or underestimated marks;

• feigned praise without personality meaningful participation, ignoring;

• lack of positive emotions in the family;

• lack of praise and approval;

• punishment, criticism;

• material reward as the main method of encouragement;

• deprivation of material and other benefits;

• not supply of minimum means of studies;

• lack of learning material and developmental techniques aimed at expanding the horizons of the student;

• and much more.

From this list, the topic of grading is perhaps the most acute. Carl Rogers wrote that the ideal school should not contain grades. How often an unfairly low marks provokes internal or even external discontent among students and their parents. Especially when teachers begin to engage in meticulous nagging, for example, to writing: poor handwriting and blots, general design, for which whole points are reduced. But do not forget that assessment is one of the important components of the educational process and the most important reinforcement.

Another point (in addition to inadequate assessment) that contributes to a decrease in learning efficiency, the fading of motivation and a creative approach among students — is the total control of teachers and parents.

Without the provision of some freedom, the right to choose and the right to make mistakes, children feel a forced unfriendly character in gaining knowledge and either spontaneously adjust to the system, or passively or actively protest against to work in such imposed on them format. On the contrary, positive emotions, free not squeezed conversations, increase motivation and develop mental operations, communication skills, the desire to take an active part in the discussion of the lesson, improvise and even joke.

Grades and control are stressful factors for all participants in the educational process. Unfortunately, they are an integral part of it and in order for the learning to be more welcoming, are needed reinforcements and stimulus (distinctive than grades).

The presence of rewards and punishments as the main positive and negative reinforcement in the family is another controversy in Psychology. As parents, we are obliged to reward our children for good behavior and learning progress, and also bring up them according to accepted etiquette and cultural values. The questions: is how to do it correctly and is it possible to use

only praise and approval in the form of words and a friendly attitude, or is it necessary material rewards (money, toys, sweets)?

Of course, for a harmonious relationship, one should not resort to strict restrictions, it all depends on the specific family. And certainly from the presence or absence of interest and motivation. For this type of interaction, it is necessary to use such a concept introduced by neo-behaviorists as *reinforcement*.

Graduate of Harvard University, Burrhus Frederic Skinner (U.S.A.) was a follower of the behavioral ideas that a stimulus generates a reaction, that is, our behavior depends on the irritant. Together with his colleagues, he added another component to this scheme — reinforcement. B. F. Skinner developed the Theory of Operant Conditioning, the essence of which is that the necessary behavior must be reinforced either positively in the form of food (social approval), or in the form of canceling negative reinforcement (social rejection).

Reinforcement is an important part of learning and teaching. In order to develop cognitive activity, it is necessary to use creative reinforcement.

For example: how better to please the child for progress in studies than to offer him a toy, chocolate or money; or like that: you have progress on the subject of History, then in our free time we will go together to the Historical Museum, and also see and buy a new book about the life of famous people.

In practice, it turns out that both methods work, but positive learning motivation can be more ramified, deep and stable when it is based on affirmations: I study not only for grades and not for that my parents to download a new game for me, but for my own development, self-actualization.

There is nothing better than the kind of motivation which

have a students with true, cognitive and creative activity, responsibility and confidence in their abilities and that teachers and parents are interested in their success and therefore support and reinforcement educational progress with good reports, awards and gifts.

A positive attitude is very important in everything, including education. It is bad and wrong when negative motivation used with negative reinforcement, usually having form of intimidation. For example, if you bring an unsatisfactory mark and will behave badly, you won't get a computer and will stay in your room.

It must be remembered that a child can unconditionally follow your orders for fear of punishment, but he will not be sincere and affectionate with you for a long time. It is much better when he fulfills your requests in order to be useful in a family where he is supported and loved.

On an example my family, I will say that on my kids as a reinforcement well works: for the son, completed homework, then can play on the computer, and for the daughter, sweets are a prerequisite for a good relationship. I call it two-way reinforcement.

On the one hand, my son's computer is a device for entertainment, on the other hand, it is a tool that is designed to search for educational information, network communication, and creativity.

For my daughter, on the one hand, chocolate is a dessert, and on the other hand, it is a product that contains happiness hormones (serotonin and endorphins) and flavonoid substances that stimulate brain activity and thereby improve mood, memory and learning progress.

Of course, these examples show the desire to create a

favorable atmosphere in the family with the help of fairly simple things.

If we talk about money as a material reinforcement, then for schoolchildren it has weak motivation and works only at the beginning. Such an stimulus diminishes rapidly and cannot sustain success in an activity all the time. If a young person is not interested or difficult to carry out family and school assignments, then no amount of money will not increase his result, most likely on the contrary, a reward for a job that you don't like or don't really understand why you need it, will not bring satisfaction and cause irritation and rejection.

Of course, teenagers need pocket money, they must learn financial literacy and manage it. It's just dangerous to use financial reinforcement in studies. In this case, it turns out that the child has been working since childhood, and studies is viewed (by adults and children) as a tool for earning money, which replaces the main purpose of learning.

Let us dwell on the general patterns that are involved in the formation of positive or negative motivation in students.

Firstly, these are external sources:

• the presence of a school, educational programs, equipment (more globally, this is generally an opportunity to get an education);

• expectations — society waiting results from the funds spent on education, and students waiting from the school to acquire knowledge for further full development;

• requirements — compliance with social norms of behavior and communication, depending on the culture and country where the student is studying.

Secondly, these are internal sources characterized by individual interests and cognitive needs leading to self-

development, self-realization (actualization) and social approval:
  • personal characteristics — an important place is occupied by the personality of the student, his age, intellectual development and abilities, self-esteem, character (introvert, extrovert or neurotic, etc.), and external signs.

Diagnostics of personal characteristics
  • The Eysenck Personality Inventory (EPI), H. Eysenck — original version, later versions (EPQ), (EPP);
  • The Sixteen Personality Factor Questionnaire (16PF), R. Cattell — (14PF) for 12–18 years old; (12PF) for 8–12 years old;
  • The Freiburger Persönlichkeitsinventar (FPI), J. Fahrenberg, H. Selg — contains questions regarding way of behavior in various situations, there is also (FPI–Revised);
  • The Keirsey Temperament Sorter (KTS), D. Keirsey — a method for determining the type of temperament, which helps to compose a psychological portrait (extraversion/introversion; sensing/intuition; thinking/feeling; judging/perceiving);
  • The Emotional Intelligence Self-Evaluation (EQ), Nicholas Hall — consists of five scales: emotional awareness, managing your emotions, self-motivation, empathy, managing the emotions of other people.

It is believed that learning activities are more effective when the student has internal motivation, thanks to which he receives positive emotions and satisfaction from his work. Even difficult tasks are solved more productively if they acquire the status of personally significant ones (this is about what wrote D. B. Elkonin).

Relying only on external motives, for example, assessment or monetary reward, the student experiences anxiety and emotional tension, which leads to a decrease in learning results,

because he does not fully use all the necessary mechanisms such as attention, memory, control. He is not very interested in complex tasks that require special efforts, since the main purpose is superficial knowledge, a certain minimum is only to receive a reward. And as soon as it is received, the activity ceases to be interesting and motivated.

However, it is the tasks of increased complexity that make the educational process more exciting. J. W. Atkinson put forward the following hypothesis: the higher the probability of success, the less excitement: if the chance of passing the exam is ten percent, then the excitement is ninety percent. On the contrary, if the chance of passing the exam is eighty percent, it is easy and does not cause an emotional reaction.

I am deeply convinced that educational activities will only when be beneficial and joyful if the teacher can determine the optimal difficulty of tasks for everyone, both for those who are lagging behind the program and for students with a high level of intelligence.

Working with gifted children is also difficult and requires certain skills. The opposite problem arises — tasks designed for the average student for lagging children turn out to be difficult, and for gifted ones too easy, and they do not contribute to the development of learning motivation.

A separate task facing the teacher is the early identification of students who are successful in their studies. This is where there is an area for the application of problem-development learning, project methods and the activity-based approach.

There is another group of gifted students — they do not show high grades in school subjects, but have creative talents in painting, music, literature, acting…

Often, genius people have mental characteristics that do not

fit into the life of an ordinary person, they otherwise perceive this world and are unable to the knowledge of school disciplines. So, the Danish writer Hans Christian Andersen thanks to school rejection could not master the literacy of writing in time, nevertheless he became a famous storyteller on all over the world.

For this group of children, it is necessary to have an individually developed curriculum, offer them participation in various Olympiads, competitions. Here, like nowhere else, is needed a free upbringing school, since genius children are very freedom-loving and spontaneous, they hardly obey generally accepted school rules which annoy and neuroticize them, preventing focusing on the main thing. If a regular school cannot match their level of mastering of information, then needs to be introduced an additional specialized education.

Observation and diagnostics of motivation

Even within one lesson, there are three stages of motivation:

• initial motivation — an introduction to the subject of study, where it is necessary to interest students in the topic of discussion;

• current motivation — maintaining interest and further presentation of the material;

• final motivation — summing up and building plans for further interaction in the next lesson.

Teachers are faced with the difficult task of keeping track of pupils' interest in the educational process in time; which subjects and topics are active and which do not. You know, what upsets teachers the most in their lessons it is not disobedience and talking, but boring, yawning faces of students.

In addition to observation, you can use profile

questionnaires; have students write a short essay to identify in more detail the dominant external and internal learning motives. In elementary school, I used a questionnaire and a drawing test by L. N. Blinova, on the topic: What do I like at school? The test turned out to be quite informative. For high school students were offered methods: Studying the Attitude to Academic Subjects by G. N. Kazantseva and Studying the Directionality on the Acquisition of Knowledge by E. P. Ilyin, N. A. Kurdyukova.

In work, the teacher always has to take into account the entire range of motives, because in addition to the main cognitive, there are always to some extent social motives, motives of achievement success and avoidance of failures and punishments.

Motivation, this is a secret!

For example, to a direct question: Do you like school? Most likely the school psychologist will receive a socially approved answer from the student.

Research of motivational sphere refers to the emotional–personal theme.

Consequently, when testing people using questionnaires, there is a high level of probability that the results will have errors associated with false answers, misinterpretation and calculation of the correlation coefficient. Therefore personality questionnaires need to be supported by other diagnostic methods (projection, observation, interview).

A more difficult problem is hidden in the analysis of the unconscious, because many motives are not always represented in consciousness. Sigmund Freud emphasized that a conscious desire does not always have a conscious purpose.

If to try to explain it in a simpler way, a good example will be computer flash memory. Initially, it contains only service

information necessary for normal operation. In process of use occurs cycles, read/write data. Under certain conditions, deleted data can be recovered.

The human brain is much more complex, but nevertheless it also has zones of used and it is logical to assume and clean (unused zones of memory).

Zones of memory where information was not previously stored, most likely, cannot convey to our consciousness some kind of unconscious, due to the lack of information.

But in other zones of memory, where we remembered real and abstract information (processed and modified by our brain), and subsequently left unattended for an indefinite time (without direct conscious appeal to it), it is quite possible to transfer the unconscious, which together or separately with the conscious to drives us.

From a practical point of view, after this brief overview of the origins of our consciousness, it will be necessary to consider the issues of adolescent life uncertainty and lack of desire to learn.

Let's start with examples:

• families with a sufficient level of income, where children show poor learning progress due to the abundance of all boon. Comfortable living conditions do not cause the desire for self-development and education, that is strange. With such resources it should be interesting to live, study and work in a creative way, but apparently not for some of them!

• families in which parents have a high status, academic degree, fame, and their children are not aimed at learning for reasons of unwillingness to compete with parents and the awareness that they cannot achieve such results.

• families where children have heightened demands for

life to achieve which they do not make their own efforts. They are driven by an infantile statement: get it all or nothing. Interest in the world around will show only after a hypothetical phenomenal success with the help of luck or an unknown/well-known sponsor.

• families living in underdeveloped regions or families with a limited budget, where children know exactly what profession they want to study, but the general life situation does not provide such an opportunity. Adolescents experience frustration, which takes away their learning motivation and introduces them into uncertainty because dreams are crumbling and there is nothing to replace them.

These examples show that not all adolescents act rationally for their future.

Laziness, low self-esteem, frustration, lack of persistence is the first thing that interferes with the formation of learning motivation and discourages the desire to studies.

V. V. Davydov noted that the problem of the mass school is not that the student has no interest in subjects, but that he has no interest in himself as a personality. In this regard, D. B. Elkonin and V. V. Davydov developed a method of *developmental education*, described earlier, where learning activity is experienced by a child not as a monotonous everyday routine, but as everyday discoveries (opening oneself and one's capabilities).

About this wrote C. Rogers and A. Maslow, calling it *self-actualization*. This technique can also be used when working with lost students: Do you know what the essence of the fact that you go to school and listen to boring subjects there? The fact that it contributes to your self-development and growth, makes your life conscious and opens up different sides of self-improvement.

Erik H. Erikson in his own Theory of Personality described

eight life-stages in which there is a stage related to adolescent development and where is indicated loss of self-identification in young people. He saw the cause for this in a difficult inharmonious childhood, when a teenager is not able to determine in myself true I (who am I), which manifests in the complexity of determining role attitudes, them gradation. With an unfavorable course of this adolescent crisis, can form a pathological identification, which will manifest in protests and negativism, this is what we have already described earlier.

Therefore, in order not to bring the situation to such a result, need to actively search how to interest the student for cognition. Here are welcomed quickness and freshness of ideas.

Learning without motivation is possible, but is it interesting, this is a big question?

Definitely, you can give examples from the life of parents, relatives, famous people of how they achieved success, but this is usually perceived neutrally by teenagers who have lost confidence and interest in learning. A good incentive can be friendly communication with students of higher educational Institutions. Also introduce your children's to science and the humanities subjects through periodical journals, multimedia (TV, Internet), conference, creative programs and etc. Invite tutors in some subjects (no more than two or three in one year) in order to improve knowledge other than the school curriculum.

If a student stubbornly avoids learning, then creativity will help him, which must be considered as a tool for cognition of science. For example, if science fiction is interesting, then we can talk about astronomy, and then explain that it, in turn, requires knowledge of related disciplines (mathematics, physics, chemistry…).

Look together with your child where he is intellectually

skidding and for whatever cause he cannot move forward. This requires a frank conversation, sometimes outside help.

In adolescence, one of the crucial moments is the question of choosing a future profession. It is very good when a person knows exactly who he wants to become and purposefully goes to the realization of this dream.

Teenagers, with difficulties in self-determination, we advise to pass various tests for career guidance, as well as familiarize with the practical side of different professions in order to make the right choice, taking into account many factors, starting with what abilities and opportunities are available, and ending with the demand for vacancies in the labor market.

You know, in my youth I dreamed of becoming an actress. But everything was decided when I had a meaningful conversation with my relative (stage director at theater). And she revealed to me not very attractive conditions for acting work, where the main problem is lack of demand. This raises the question, what to do next with this diploma if it has no practical application.

So dreams are great, but be careful so that desires coincide with realities, specifically here and now in this rapidly changing world.

In life, you need to have reserve options so as not to be left behind.

Studies are a ticket to adulthood, and it is necessary not only for mastering any profession, but also for the general development of all components — intellect, spiritual and cultural values, physical development in a healthy body a healthy mind.

The results show that only fifteen percent of school graduates can be attributed to a practically healthy category (this indicator varies from country to country).

Over the past decades, there has been a shift in priorities in favor of scientific disciplines. This increased the burden on children. Even in the school timetable for GCSE high school students, we are seeing a decline in sports activities to one per week. They don't have time for sports because they have to pay more attention to lessons.

Developing new quality programs in education, it is also necessary to introduce methods aimed at strengthening the health of students.

Diagnostics of motivation

The motivational components is investigated using questionnaires, observation and specialized tests:

• The Mehrabian Achieving Tendency Scale (MATS), A. Mehrabian — scale of motivational achievements (the motive of striving for success and the motive avoidance of failure) for high school students;

• Resultant Achievement Motivation (RAM), A. Mehrabian — based on Theory of Achievement Motivation, by J. W. Atkinson;

• Methodology for diagnosing personality for Motivation to Avoid Failures (MAF), T. Ehlers;

• Locus of Control (LOC), J. B. Rotter — cognitive orientation for students; determines how a person reacts to events in life, referring to external circumstances or internal personal causes;

• The Thematic Apperception Test (TAT), H. Heckhausen — projective method research of achievement motivation for adults;

• The Crowne–Marlowe Social Desirability Scale, D. P. Crowne, D. Marlowe — scale that measures a person's need for approval by others;

• The Edwards Personal Preference Schedule (EPPS), A.

L. Edwards — based on Theory of the Human Needs, by H. A. Murray, identifies basic needs and motives (for ages 16 and up);

• Methodology Value Orientations, M. Rokich — explores the orientation of the personality, the system of value orientations and motivational life activity;

• The Self-Directed Search (SDS), J. Holland — a questionnaire that allows to identify the compatibility of the social orientation of the personality with the professional environment (realistic, investigative, artistic, social, enterprising, conventional).

Conclusion

We have come to the end of our review of what modern education should be. On the pages of this book was described the history of the emergence and development of pedagogy, the main names involved in the formation of learning methods, pedagogical tasks and functions, types of schools; is separately touched upon the topic of personal characteristics of the teacher and emotional burnout. And of course the most important — were considered the difficulties with which faced by students, teachers, parents, psychologists. Also was proposed recommendations for the elimination and correction of various obstacles among students in order to overcome and improve the quality of education.

In conclusion of this topic, I want to say that difficulties in learning (cognition) are present in our life with a double message, in order to overcome them and develop further.

A student attending school without meaning, without motive, without purpose is a student who is lost in time.

The well-known psychologist Erik H. Erikson in self Theory of Personality argued that person develops throughout life, the main purpose of which is to find own *ego identity*, that is, a vocation, a purpose, to collect one's own image of I into a single whole.

Humanists will tell us that a happy person is a person with self-actualization (personal self-realization).

According to Sigmund Freud, will have to lie down for several months, or even years, on the couch of a psychoanalyst,

what would get to the unconscious and get rid of the protective mechanisms of the psyche; and according to A. Adler — from an inferiority complex.

Abraham Maslow at one time put self-actualization at the top of the pyramid of human needs as his highest purpose.

The logotherapist Viktor Frankl, in his Man's Search for Meaning of life speaking about self-actualization, noted that this is not the ultimate destiny of a person, not his primary aspiration. Like happiness, self-actualization will appear itself in the process of implementation of sense. Only with the implementation of the sense which located in the external world human realize himself as a personality.

My favorite phrase in what is the meaning of life is a simple truth: to live reasonably. But for this need to learn all your life. There is no necessary to wait until the end of school, then the college or university, and that's all, finally, freedom, without learning, without difficulties.

In today's changing world, the need for the desire and ability to learn is growing every year.

The idea of lifelong learning emerged in the 1960s as a response to changes in all spheres of human life: production, socio-economic component, the development of new high and nano technologies, IT industry, which affected all areas, starting with a travel ticket, banking services, shopping and ending with interpersonal communication, acquaintances and of course, education.

For this cause, the school changed its purpose, it became a start for further learning and self-development.

Now the school, in addition to scientific disciplines, must develop the ability and motivation for self-education; to teach: flexible and creative thinking, teamwork, communication with

different age and professional categories of people, the basics of life safety and a healthy lifestyle.

In the senior classes, is actual to preparation for final exams, certification and ceremonial graduation from school. In the best traditions, students should have positive memories of school and the passed stages of education, of participation in bright events and responsible projects, as well as of the people who accompanied them.

I wish you creativity and new discoveries!

About the Author

Tatiana Semenova is a practical psychologist and a teacher of psychology. Her specialization is in clinical psychology. She graduated from the Institute of Psychology and Pedagogy, Moscow. She also graduated from Moscow Medical College No. 1 with a specialization in nursing (generalist nurse). She worked at the Scientific Research Institute of Transplantology and Artificial Organs in the Department of Rhythm Disorders, Cardiac Surgery and Assisted Circulation. She completed practice in psychiatry, neurology and defectology in state institutions. She had an internship at a public and private school in the Moscow region.